Into the Dark Web: True Crimes and Secrets of the Hidden Internet

Manuel P is an author specializing in **true crime**, **personal security**, and **survival**, with a passion for exploring the fine line between danger and human resilience. Through his works, he combines gripping storytelling with practical insights, equipping readers with the tools they need to understand and navigate critical situations.

His **true crime** books delve into real-life stories of modern crimes, uncovering the darkest details of criminal psychology and the investigative processes that lead to justice. In his guides on **security and survival**, Manuel P provides valuable advice and strategies grounded in thorough research and real-world scenarios, making them ideal for anyone seeking to be prepared for life's unexpected challenges.

With a straightforward and accessible style, Manuel P appeals to both fans of crime and mystery and those looking to enhance their awareness and ability to respond to unpredictable events.

INTRODUCTION

There was a faint glow on the laptop screen. A window opened to nothingness, yet brimming with promises. A man sat alone in the dark, staring at the anonymous interface of the Tor browser. Here, in the silence of his room, he felt powerful: a gateway to a parallel universe where no one knew his name, where the rules of the real world faded away.

This is the Dark Web, the hidden side of the internet. A place many imagine as a shadowy marketplace for criminal activity, but also a refuge for journalists, political dissidents, and activists seeking freedom of expression. It is here that humanity's darkest impulses find fertile ground, masked by an anonymity that seems impenetrable.

To understand what the Dark Web is, we must first distinguish it from the Deep Web. Picture the internet as an iceberg: the surface, where we navigate daily, is the visible part. The Deep Web is the vast submerged mass, made up of databases, archives, and information not indexed by search engines. The Dark Web, however, lies even deeper: an encrypted network accessible only through specific tools, such as Tor.

Originally created for legitimate purposes, such as ensuring privacy in oppressive regimes, the Dark Web quickly attracted criminals of all kinds: pedophiles, drug dealers, fraudsters, and even murderers. Yet even here, where anonymity reigns supreme, traces are never entirely erased.

This book tells the stories of people and crimes that found their stage on the Dark Web. True stories, often harrowing, that reveal the devastating impact of these activities on victims' lives. It is not

just a journey into horror, but a warning: even the darkest web cannot guarantee absolute silence.

PedoBook: The Dark Side of Virtual Communities

Introduction: A Case That Shocked the World

It was a quiet morning in 2015 when an agent of the Italian Postal Police, while conducting a routine investigation into the trafficking of illegal images, stumbled upon something shocking. A forum hidden deep within the Dark Web revealed traces of a far more organized operation than anyone had imagined. Those few lines of code, concealed behind layers of encryption, were the gateway to PedoBook, a dark platform dedicated to the exchange of images, videos, and horrifying content that glorified the abuse of minors.

At first glance, PedoBook seemed like just another forum on the Dark Web, but it was

much more. It was a fully-fledged "social network" for pedophiles, complete with user profiles, thematic sections, discussion forums, and even a ranking system based on the contribution of illegal material. What shocked authorities was not only the technological sophistication of the platform but also its global reach: thousands of users from all corners of the world logged in daily to participate in this collective horror.

PedoBook epitomizes the darkest side of technological evolution, where anonymity and encryption become tools to perpetrate unspeakable crimes. Its discovery raised profound questions: How could a platform of such scale exist undetected? What gaps in international legislation and technological surveillance allowed its proliferation?

This is the story of an investigation that took years of effort and the collaboration of dozens of international agencies, culminating in the dismantling of one of

the most dangerous networks ever uncovered on the Dark Web. But it is also the story of a system that continues to evolve, adapting to authorities' attempts to shut it down, and of victims whose suffering can never be erased.

By following the PedoBook case, we will not only recount the events but also delve into the moral, technological, and cultural implications of a battle that is far from over.

The Origins of PedoBook

The Birth of a Shadow on the Web

PedoBook emerged in the early 2010s, during a time when the Dark Web was gaining notoriety as an anonymous and unregulated digital space. Fueled by the rise of tools like the Tor browser and the growing use of cryptocurrencies, the Dark Web became a fertile ground for illegal activities. It was within this context that a small group of individuals, highly skilled in

cybersecurity and cryptography, decided to create a platform designed to host illegal content related to child abuse.

A Platform Like No Other

Unlike other hidden forums, PedoBook was not just a simple sharing space. It presented itself as a full-fledged "social network" for pedophiles, with a design reminiscent of mainstream platforms. Users could create profiles, participate in thematic discussions, exchange content, and even gain "status" based on their contributions to the community.

The key features of PedoBook included:

Exclusive Access: Membership was granted only through direct invitations and verification. Aspiring members had to prove their "trustworthiness" by sharing illegal content as evidence.

Organized Structure: The platform was divided into thematic sections, private

forums, and closed groups, each with specific rules and administrators ensuring their functionality.

Advanced Security: PedoBook employed end-to-end encryption to protect communications and accepted only cryptocurrency payments, making transactions difficult to trace.

Who Was Behind It?

Subsequent investigations revealed that PedoBook was managed by a small group of individuals with advanced skills in cybersecurity and hacking. Some of them were already known to authorities for similar crimes but had evaded capture by exploiting gaps in international legislation and the anonymity provided by the Dark Web. These individuals were motivated not only by financial gain but also by a twisted ideology that sought to normalize the crimes promoted by the platform.

Initial Growth

PedoBook started with a limited number of members, but word of mouth within pedophile communities contributed to rapid growth. Thanks to its innovative structure and promise of absolute anonymity, the platform attracted users from around the world. Within a few years, PedoBook boasted thousands of active members, becoming one of the largest hubs for exchanging illegal content on the Dark Web.

The platform's exponential growth did not go unnoticed. Authorities began monitoring suspicious activities linked to PedoBook, laying the groundwork for an investigation that would take years to complete.

Recruitment and Expansion of PedoBook

A System Built on Trust

The success of PedoBook was not only due to its technological infrastructure but also

to an ingeniously designed recruitment system. To ensure security and maintain trust among members, the platform's administrators implemented an exclusive access model that guaranteed every new user was a "valuable contribution" to the community.

Invitation System: Access to PedoBook was granted exclusively through personal invitations from active members. These invitations were issued only after thorough verification of the candidate, who had to prove their "worth" by providing illegal content as evidence.

Trust Tests: To pass the initial screening, new users had to complete a series of tests designed to demonstrate their involvement and adherence to the platform's "rules." These tests included sharing illicit material or participating in specific discussions within forums.

Internal Hierarchy: The platform was structured with a hierarchical system that

rewarded the most active members. Users could gain "status" and access reserved sections by regularly contributing new content.

International Spread

Once a base of trusted users was established, PedoBook rapidly expanded through word of mouth and internal propaganda. Active members promoted the platform in other corners of the Dark Web, attracting new users with the promise of absolute anonymity and access to exclusive content.

Recruitment Forums: Other forums on the Dark Web served as indirect recruitment channels. Here, users affiliated with PedoBook left cryptic clues and information to guide potential new members to the platform.

Premium Content: PedoBook incentivized participation by offering "premium" content to those who demonstrated their

commitment through regular contributions. This model reinforced user dependency on the platform and ensured its continuous growth.

Global Network: Within a few years, PedoBook boasted members from every corner of the globe. This global network made the platform not only a hub for content exchange but also a meeting point for collaboration among criminals.

Normalization of Abuse

One of the most disturbing aspects of PedoBook was its ability to normalize the crimes it promoted. Through forums and thematic groups, administrators and influential users propagated a narrative that justified child abuse as acceptable or even "natural." This propaganda mechanism not only attracted new members but also created an ideological bubble where crimes were minimized or celebrated.

administrators' ability to quickly adapt to new threats. However, the seeds of its downfall had already been planted.

The Impact on PedoBook's Victims

Invisible Victims of a Global Network

PedoBook was not merely a platform for sharing illegal content but a system that fueled a vicious cycle of abuse and exploitation. The victims, often children aged between 3 and 12, were recruited through various channels, ranging from manipulation on social media to exploitation within their own homes. Behind every image and video shared, there were stories of pain, fear, and lasting trauma.

Methods of Grooming

PedoBook users employed sophisticated strategies to groom their victims, exploiting children's vulnerabilities and,

in some cases, relying on the complicity of adults.

Social Media as a Hunting Ground: Platforms like Facebook, Instagram, and TikTok were used to approach children. Predators, often posing as peers or using fake accounts, built trust before exploiting it to obtain private photos and videos.

Infiltration of Online Communities: Criminals frequented groups and forums popular with young people, offering false opportunities such as modeling auditions or fake job offers.

Familial Complicity: In some cases, content was produced directly by family members who exploited their own children for financial gain or to satisfy specific requests from other platform users.

The Spiral of Abuse

Once initial material was obtained, victims were often trapped in a cycle of abuse and blackmail:

Emotional Blackmail: Predators threatened to share the collected images or videos, forcing victims to produce additional material.

Isolation: Victims often felt unable to confide in anyone, fearing judgment or repercussions.

Escalation of Abuse: The growing demand for increasingly extreme content drove predators to push victims into progressively degrading situations.

Long-Term Psychological Consequences

The psychological impact on victims was devastating, with effects that often lasted a lifetime:

Post-Traumatic Stress Disorder (PTSD): Many children developed symptoms such as

recurring nightmares, panic attacks, and flashbacks related to their abuse.

Chronic Anxiety and Depression: The constant fear of being exposed or judged made it difficult for victims to lead normal lives.

Relational Issues: Many survivors struggled to trust others, developing a distorted perception of interpersonal relationships.

The Difficulty of Breaking the Silence

Reporting abuse was often an almost impossible step for victims. Shame, fear of not being believed, and, in some cases, lack of support from their families contributed to their silence. Even when reports were made, the path to recovery was long and challenging, often hindered by a lack of resources and specialists capable of addressing the trauma linked to this type of abuse.

A Persistent Problem

Despite the dismantling of PedoBook, the problem of online child exploitation remains a global scourge. Every day, new platforms emerge that seek to replicate PedoBook's model, demonstrating that the fight against these crimes is far from over.

Tackling this challenge requires not only a constant commitment from authorities but also increased awareness and sensitivity from society to protect its most vulnerable members.

Investigations: An Unprecedented Operation

The Beginning of the Investigation

The investigation into PedoBook began almost by chance when an agent from the Italian Postal Police detected an unusual data exchange on a Dark Web forum. Initially thought to be an isolated case,

this lead uncovered a well-organized network operating in secrecy. What appeared to be a small group of users turned out to be a global platform with thousands of active members.

International Collaboration

Due to PedoBook's international reach, Italian authorities quickly realized that the investigation would require global coordination. Interpol, Europol, and various national police forces joined together to tackle the operation.

Information Sharing: Using shared platforms, law enforcement agencies began identifying users and linking their activities to other ongoing investigations.

Advanced Technologies: Cryptocurrency tracking software, data traffic analysis tools, and de-anonymization techniques were used to trace PedoBook's administrators.

Undercover Operations: Infiltrated agents posed as users on the platform to gather incriminating evidence and map the network.

Challenges Faced

Despite the resources at their disposal, authorities encountered numerous obstacles during the investigation:

Anonymity of the Dark Web: The use of the Tor browser and cryptocurrencies made it extremely difficult to trace users' real identities.

Codes and Cryptic Language: PedoBook users employed specific jargon to prevent their conversations from being understood by outsiders.

Frequent Relocations: The platform's administrators frequently changed servers and domains to evade detection.

The Breakthrough

The breakthrough came when one of the main administrators made a human error. During a cryptocurrency transaction, they used a centralized exchange that required identity verification. This small mistake allowed investigators to link the anonymous account to a real individual, paving the way to dismantle the entire network.

A Global Operation

With the information collected, authorities launched a coordinated international operation. Arrests were made in multiple countries, and servers containing terabytes of illegal material were seized. This operation not only led to the shutdown of PedoBook but also to the identification and rescue of numerous victims.

The Dismantling and Legal Consequences

The Final Operation

After years of complex investigations and international collaboration, law enforcement agencies were ready to strike. The final operation against PedoBook was launched simultaneously across multiple countries, coordinated by Europol and Interpol. The primary objectives were to dismantle the platform, arrest its administrators, and identify its most active users while ensuring the protection of identified victims.

Coordinated Arrests: Dozens of individuals were arrested in countries including Italy, the United States, Germany, and Australia. Among those arrested were not only regular users but also administrators and moderators of the platform.

Server Seizure: PedoBook's servers, which had been distributed across various locations to avoid detection, were located and seized. This allowed authorities to

collect crucial evidence, including user activity logs and shared content.

Victim Rescue: Information gathered during the operation led to the identification and rescue of dozens of minors involved in the abuse. The victims were provided psychological support and assisted through a lengthy rehabilitation process.

Trials and Sentences

Following the dismantling of PedoBook, a series of lengthy judicial proceedings began. The defendants included administrators, active users, and individuals who had used the platform to commission abuse.

Charges: The accused faced severe charges, including the production and distribution of child exploitation material, child abuse, and participation in a criminal organization.

Overwhelming Evidence: Thanks to the data retrieved from the servers, authorities had irrefutable proof, including conversation records, cryptocurrency transactions, and shared content.

Harsh Sentences: Many defendants received extremely severe penalties, with sentences ranging from 10 years to life imprisonment in the most egregious cases.

Legal and Social Impact

The dismantling of PedoBook had significant repercussions both legally and socially:

New Legislation: Many countries introduced or strengthened laws to combat online sexual exploitation and improve international cooperation in investigating digital crimes.

Increased Awareness: The PedoBook case brought global attention to the scale of online child exploitation, raising public

awareness about the importance of digital safety and protecting the most vulnerable.

Prevention Initiatives: Non-profits and governments launched campaigns to educate parents, teachers, and children about the dangers of online grooming and the importance of reporting suspicious activities.

An Evolving System

Despite the operation's success, the PedoBook case represented only a partial victory. Illegal platforms continue to proliferate on the Dark Web, evolving to evade law enforcement controls. The fight against online sexual exploitation is far from over, requiring constant effort from governments, law enforcement, and civil society.

The dismantling of PedoBook, however, remains a testament to how international cooperation and collective commitment can yield significant results in combating some of the most heinous crimes.

Conclusion: A Partial Victory in the Fight Against Online Crime

The PedoBook case marked a milestone in the fight against online sexual exploitation, demonstrating how international collaboration and investigative technologies can yield significant results. The dismantling of such a complex global network not only brought an end to one of the most dangerous platforms on the Dark Web but also rescued dozens of victims and exposed gaps in surveillance systems and legislation.

However, this victory is only partial. Shutting down PedoBook did not stop the proliferation of similar platforms. Every day, new networks emerge, adapting to countermeasures and using increasingly advanced technologies to maintain anonymity and evade authorities.

Lessons Learned and the Future of the Fight

The PedoBook case provided crucial lessons:

The Importance of International Collaboration: Only through global coordination can criminal networks operating without borders be tackled.

Evolving Investigative Techniques: Law enforcement must continuously update their skills to keep pace with the technological innovations used by criminals.

Societal Awareness: Prevention is key. Educating families, young people, and professionals is essential to identify and report the dangers of grooming and online exploitation.

A Message of Hope

Despite the challenges, the PedoBook case demonstrates that justice can be achieved and victims can be protected. Every arrest and every dismantled network is a step towards a safer internet and a more aware

society. The battle is long and complex, but the determination of authorities and the support of the global community are powerful tools to combat these crimes.

The story of PedoBook is both a warning and a call to action. Technology should not only be a tool of oppression and abuse but also a means to create a future where the most vulnerable are protected and perpetrators are held accountable.

Matthew Falder

The Brilliant Academic with a Dark Side

Matthew Falder seemed to have it all: intelligence, success, and a promising academic career. Born into a middle-class family, he had shown a brilliant mind and an insatiable curiosity for science from an early age. At school, he excelled in every subject, but his true passion was geology. His teachers described him as a reserved but ambitious student, capable of earning the respect of his peers through determination and talent.

After high school, Falder earned a scholarship to attend the University of Cambridge, one of the most prestigious institutions in the world. There, he fully immersed himself in his field of study, earning the admiration of his professors and colleagues. He published high-level

scientific papers and contributed to innovative research projects. On the surface, his life seemed to be a testament to discipline and success.

But behind this impeccable facade lay a dark side that no one suspected. Falder led a double life, hiding his darkest impulses from everyone, including his closest friends. He spent countless hours in front of his computer, exploring the Dark Web and building a secret identity that allowed him to indulge his most perverse instincts.

In his academic life, Falder was known for his reserved nature. He rarely attended social events and preferred to spend his free time alone. To those who knew him, this behavior seemed normal: "He's just an introvert," his colleagues would say. No one imagined that this solitude was the fertile ground for a mind increasingly consumed by darkness.

The Dark Web was his playground, a realm where he could act without fear of being

discovered. Using pseudonyms and tools to mask his identity, he began frequenting secret forums, exploring illicit content and forging connections with others who shared his deviant interests. But Falder was not just a passive consumer: he quickly became an active player, contributing content and developing strategies to manipulate his victims.

This dark side, completely invisible in daylight, stood in stark contrast to the public image Falder projected. Friends and colleagues remembered him as a brilliant but distant person, a man who spoke little about himself and much about his professional ambitions. He was a master of concealment, skilled at building an impenetrable barrier between his two lives.

His Modus Operandi and His Victims

The way Matthew Falder selected, manipulated, and exploited his victims was as methodical as it was chilling. His

ability to identify vulnerabilities and build a bond of trust only to psychologically destroy his prey was the hallmark of his criminal activity.

Falder regularly frequented social networks, online forums, and platforms where people shared personal details about their lives. He was an astute observer, able to precisely detect signs of emotional fragility. He sought out individuals with low self-esteem, those who posted melancholic messages or appeared isolated. These details, to him, were invaluable clues for selecting his victims.

The initial contact was always subtle. He used pseudonyms and fake identities, often posing as a supportive figure or someone offering opportunities. "You have a wonderful smile," he wrote to a potential victim, "have you ever thought about modeling?" This initial approach, seemingly harmless, served to put people at ease and create a sense of trust.

Once contact was established, Falder began a process of subtle but relentless manipulation. He would request innocent images, promising rewards such as money or emotional support. When the images were sent, his tone shifted dramatically. He used those photos as leverage to demand increasingly compromising content. The initial kindness turned into threats and control.

Falder created a web of fear around his victims. He threatened to share compromising images with friends, family, or colleagues, destroying their social and professional lives. For many of his victims, the shame and fear were so overwhelming that they felt there was no way out. Some were coerced into performing degrading acts, recording them, and sending them to Falder, who would then use the material for further blackmail.

His modus operandi extended beyond direct manipulation. Falder also used Dark Web forums to share content and methods with

other users. He was regarded as a prominent member of these communities, where he shared his strategies for luring, manipulating, and blackmailing victims. This criminal support network not only provided him with new ideas but also reinforced his belief in his own invincibility.

His ruthlessness was evident in the way he treated his victims. He saw them as mere tools to satisfy his perversions, devoid of dignity or worth. In intercepted conversations, Falder bragged about the control he exerted over them, describing them as "pawns" in his personal game.

An emblematic case: One of his victims was a young woman whom Falder convinced to send an innocent photo. Within months, that same woman was coerced into recording degrading videos under the threat of public exposure. This case, like many others, highlighted the systematic progression of his abuse.

The Investigations That Exposed Him

The investigation that led to Matthew Falder's capture is a remarkable example of international collaboration, investigative tenacity, and technological expertise. It all began with a series of anonymous reports from victims. These complaints, initially considered isolated cases, came from different parts of the world. However, when the details of their stories were compared, a disturbing pattern emerged.

The first critical step was identifying the Dark Web forums frequented by Falder. Using advanced digital tracking tools, investigators managed to pinpoint some of the platforms he regularly used. These forums were hidden behind encrypted networks and accessible only through the Tor browser. Within them, users shared illegal content and openly discussed exploitation techniques. Under his

pseudonyms, Falder wasn't just a participant but one of the most respected and active members of the community.

One of the main challenges for authorities was overcoming the level of anonymity provided by the technological tools Falder relied on. To do this, the UK's National Crime Agency (NCA) collaborated with Europol and international cybersecurity agencies. Every digital trace, no matter how small, was meticulously analyzed. The breakthrough came when investigators discovered a technical error: an IP address not fully masked that linked one of his online activities to a physical location in the UK.

With this lead, investigators began monitoring Falder's communications, gathering evidence that connected his online pseudonyms to his real identity. At the same time, they started reconstructing the network of his victims, collecting testimonies and documenting the extent of his crimes. The details that emerged from

the investigation were shocking: over 200 identified victims, with cases ranging from blackmail to the distribution of extremely humiliating images and videos.

The operation to arrest him was meticulously planned. NCA agents raided his residence in a coordinated operation in 2017. Inside, they found overwhelming evidence: hard drives filled with illegal material, saved conversations, and a detailed list of his victims. The seized material required weeks of analysis to fully understand the scope of his activities.

Falder's arrest was a pivotal moment but not the conclusion. During the trial, a psychological profile emerged of a man devoid of empathy, an individual who thrived on the suffering of others. Investigators detailed his ruthlessness, while victims recounted stories of humiliation and fear that left the court stunned.

The Trial and the Impact of His Crimes

The trial of Matthew Falder was an event that shocked public opinion and highlighted the horrific consequences of his crimes. The hearings, which began shortly after his arrest in 2017, revealed a level of cruelty and manipulation few could have imagined.

During the trial, the court heard testimony from many of his victims. Young men and women tearfully recounted how Falder had destroyed their lives. Some spoke of the humiliation of having intimate images shared without their consent, while others described the helplessness they felt in succumbing to his demands under threat. Many victims reported suffering from depression, chronic anxiety, and, in some cases, suicidal thoughts due to his actions.

Investigators presented overwhelming evidence against Falder: online conversations, material recovered from his electronic devices, and expert testimony

describing the extent of his activities on the Dark Web. The court learned how he had used more than 25 pseudonyms to confuse and terrorize his victims, ensuring none could easily escape his grasp.

One of the most harrowing testimonies came from a young woman who described how Falder had manipulated every aspect of her life, making her believe she no longer had any value as a human being. "He stole my dignity, my trust, and any hope for the future," she declared in court.

When it came time for the defense, Falder remained impassive, showing no remorse for his actions. This coldness only reinforced the image of an individual devoid of empathy, driven solely by the pleasure of causing pain.

The sentence, delivered in 2018, was one of the harshest ever handed down for such crimes in the UK: 32 years in prison. The judge described Falder as a "remorseless serial predator," emphasizing the need for

an exemplary punishment to protect society and send a strong message against crimes committed through the Dark Web.

The impact of this case was significant. Not only did it bring justice to the victims, but it also sparked a public debate about online safety and the dangers of the Dark Web. Government organizations and victim advocacy groups began promoting awareness campaigns to educate the public about the risks of sharing personal information online.

The Falder case remains one of the most significant in the history of combating cybercrime. It stands as a warning about the dangers of online anonymity and the importance of global collaborations to tackle threats that know no borders.

Besa Mafia

The Myth of the Virtual Hitman

It was a dark and silent night when a man, whose name will remain unknown, sat in front of his laptop. With his heart pounding, he opened the Tor browser and ventured into the dark side of the internet. He had a clear goal: to find someone to do his dirty work. A hitman.

Navigating through encrypted links and shadowy forums, he found what he was looking for: Besa Mafia. The site promised professional assassins ready to eliminate anyone for a price. Bold letters on the homepage declared: "GUARANTEED SERVICES, PAYMENT IN BITCOIN ONLY, COMPLETE ANONYMITY." For the client, it was a dream—or a nightmare—come true.

Besa Mafia wasn't the first Dark Web site to offer murder-for-hire services, but it

was the one that gained the most attention. The name itself, a nod to Albanian "Besa," which represents honor and loyalty, lent credibility to the entire operation. It seemed like a brand designed to inspire trust, even among the most desperate criminals.

But how much of these promises were true? The legends of the Dark Web are often shrouded in mystery, and Besa Mafia was no exception. Was it really possible to hire someone to kill an enemy with just a few clicks? Or was it all part of a clever scam, exploiting people's desire for anonymity and their greed?

This is the story of Besa Mafia: a site that promised murder and revenge, but hid an even darker truth.

The Birth of a Dark Web Myth

Besa Mafia emerged on the Dark Web in early 2016, presenting itself as a professional and lethal organization. The name "Besa

Mafia" was deliberately chosen to evoke respect and fear. "Besa," in Albanian culture, represents the concept of keeping one's word and absolute loyalty. It was a brilliant branding choice, giving the site an aura of reliability in an environment where trust is a rare commodity.

The site promised to connect clients with hitmen to carry out any kind of revenge: from acts of vandalism to murder-for-hire. The homepage was simple yet compelling. A bold message dominated the screen: "NO QUESTIONS ASKED, WE GET THE JOB DONE."

According to the site's narrative, the organization boasted a network of professional assassins ready to eliminate anyone for the right price. Payments, strictly in Bitcoin, guaranteed total anonymity for both clients and executors. The site even offered a guarantee: services would be completed, or the client would receive a refund. This aggressive, straightforward approach quickly made it

popular among those seeking revenge or private justice.

One intriguing aspect was the attention to detail shown by the site's operators. The platform provided detailed instructions on how to register, make payments, and submit information about targets. Everything was designed to reassure clients of the service's professionalism. The site's administrators claimed to have access to a global network of criminal professionals, based in multiple countries, but no concrete evidence was ever provided to substantiate these claims.

The legend of Besa Mafia spread quickly, fueled by the curiosity and allure that the Dark Web holds for many. Blogs, news articles, and online forums began discussing the site, further fueling the myth. However, as its notoriety grew, so did the shadows of doubt: could such an explicit site really operate undisturbed? Or was there something more deceitful behind it?

How the Site Operated

The mystery behind Besa Mafia lay in how the site operated. The platform was designed to attract customers through a combination of operational simplicity and enticing promises. The administrators had built an ostensibly professional site that perfectly masked its true nature.

Access and Registration

To access Besa Mafia, users had to use the Tor browser, the primary tool for navigating the Dark Web. Once on the site, users were required to complete a simple yet detailed registration process. New users needed to create an account with a username, password, and a security key to ensure anonymity.

Once registered, customers could browse the various sections of the site. The homepage was divided into service categories, with detailed descriptions and clear pricing. Users could request acts of vandalism,

intimidation, or even murder, with prices varying based on the complexity of the task and the target's location.

The Purchasing Process

The payment system was entirely Bitcoin-based, a cryptocurrency renowned for its security and anonymity. Users had to transfer an initial sum as a deposit to confirm the requested job. Administrators promised that the balance would only be required upon job completion.

After the initial payment, customers were required to provide details about the target. The site requested specific information: name, address, daily routine, and even photographs. These details were uploaded through an encrypted system to ensure sensitive information could not be intercepted.

Communication with Administrators

Users could communicate directly with administrators via an internal messaging system. The messages were encrypted and, according to the site's claims, automatically deleted after a certain period. This feature increased the perception of security among customers, convincing them their requests would never be uncovered.

The administrators' responses were professional and detailed. They provided updates on job progress and advised clients on how to behave to avoid suspicion. However, behind this organized facade lay a very different reality.

The Promise of Guaranteed Success

One of the most intriguing aspects of the site was its "guarantee of success." Administrators assured customers that the job would be completed within a specified time frame. If the task was not

accomplished, they promised a full refund or reassignment to another executor. This policy, combined with the professional tone, helped build an illusion of reliability that fooled many.

Customer Reviews

To bolster credibility, the site included a section dedicated to customer reviews. Users who claimed to have used Besa Mafia's services wrote testimonials praising the efficiency and discretion of the team. However, many of these reviews were likely fabricated by the administrators themselves to attract new clients.

The Scam Behind the Myth

Behind the façade of professionalism and enticing promises, Besa Mafia hid a very different reality: a cunning scam designed to exploit people's desperation and animosity. While the site promised murder-

for-hire and other illicit acts, there is no concrete evidence that any job was ever completed. In truth, Besa Mafia operated on a simple yet effective model: take the money and vanish.

The Scam in Action

Besa Mafia's modus operandi was as straightforward as it was ruthless. After luring customers with its direct language and professional presentation, the site required an initial deposit in Bitcoin. Once payment was made, customers were instructed to provide complete details about the target and to wait patiently for the job to be executed.

However, as soon as the money was transferred, communication with the administrators became vague and inconsistent. Updates were often generic, with phrases like "The job is in progress" or "Our hitman is on the right track." Eventually, customers were either

completely ignored or asked for additional payments under the pretext of unforeseen complications.

Testimonies from Scammed Customers

Several users, who remained anonymous for obvious reasons, shared their experiences on Dark Web forums. One user stated, "I paid the required deposit and provided all the details about the target. After weeks of silence, they asked for a second payment for 'additional operational expenses.' When I refused, I never heard from them again."

Another customer recounted a similar story: "The site looked legitimate. I followed all the instructions, but after paying, they sent me confusing and contradictory messages. There was no hitman, just people trying to scam me for more money."

These testimonies reveal how Besa Mafia was designed to scam its customers, exploiting

the clandestine nature of their requests to prevent them from reporting the fraud.

The Web of Deceit

A key element of the scam was the use of fake reviews to build credibility. The site's administrators posted fabricated testimonials praising the efficiency and discretion of their services. Phrases like "The job was completed in record time" or "They are absolute professionals" filled the reviews section, convincing many new clients to trust them.

Additionally, the scammers were skilled at manipulating their customers' emotions. When a client expressed doubts or frustration, the administrators responded with messages playing on fear, suggesting that the target might be suspicious or that the police were closing in.

The Dark Side of the Dark Web

The Besa Mafia scam highlights one of the darker realities of the Dark Web: it is not only a place where crimes are committed but also a fertile ground for exploiting people's vulnerability and greed. The lack of transparency and regulation makes it difficult to distinguish between reality and fiction, allowing scammers like those behind Besa Mafia to thrive.

The Investigations and the Unveiling

The investigations that uncovered the truth behind Besa Mafia showcased how law enforcement agencies can collaborate to dismantle criminal operations on the Dark Web. The Besa Mafia case began to take shape when authorities noticed an unusual flow of Bitcoin transactions linked to the site. These financial movements, combined with testimonies from scammed users, caught the attention of Europol and other international organizations.

The Digital Trail

While the Dark Web offers a high level of anonymity, no platform is completely immune to human error or technical vulnerabilities. In the case of Besa Mafia, a series of mistakes by the site's administrators provided investigators with crucial clues. One of the most significant errors was the use of an email address regularly associated with an account on a mainstream web service.

Cybersecurity experts leveraged this connection to trace the identity behind the site. Simultaneously, they monitored Bitcoin transactions linked to Besa Mafia, cross-referencing them with data collected from cryptocurrency exchanges. This meticulous work allowed them to pinpoint the origin of the funds and connect them to a physical individual.

International Collaboration

The investigations involved agencies from several countries, including the United States, the United Kingdom, and Romania. Each agency contributed unique resources and expertise. Europol coordinated the operation, ensuring information was quickly shared across jurisdictions. One of the primary challenges was overcoming the legal and technical barriers related to digital transactions and Dark Web monitoring.

The Final Operation

The arrest of Besa Mafia's main administrator occurred in 2017. The operation was meticulously planned to ensure all evidence was legally gathered and could be used in court. When agents raided the suspect's residence, they found hard drives filled with sensitive data,

including the complete customer database of Besa Mafia.

Among the evidence collected were detailed conversations between the site's administrator and clients, as well as records proving that none of the money received was ever used to complete any jobs. This material confirmed the fraudulent nature of the site and provided a comprehensive picture of Besa Mafia's operational model.

The Impact of the Investigations

The unveiling of Besa Mafia had a significant impact on the perception of the Dark Web. The case demonstrated that even the darkest platforms can be exposed through a combination of advanced technology and international collaboration. Moreover, it raised ethical questions about the behavior of the clients: many had sought to commit serious crimes but ended up as victims of a scam.

The Moral Paradox and Lessons from the Dark Web

The Besa Mafia case left behind a trail of questions that go beyond the legal and investigative aspects. On one hand, it demonstrated the vulnerability of clients willing to trust a criminal platform. On the other, it raised a difficult moral paradox: who were the real victims?

Victims or Perpetrators?

Besa Mafia's clients turned to the site with the intent of committing serious crimes, such as intimidation, vandalism, and even murder. Many were driven by desires for revenge or greed, believing the Dark Web would provide them with anonymity and impunity. However, instead of getting what they sought, they ended up being scammed. They paid substantial amounts in Bitcoin for services that were never delivered.

This creates a moral dilemma: can they be considered victims if their intentions were criminal? The answer is not straightforward. On one hand, these individuals fell prey to a scam; on the other, their involvement places them in a position of moral and legal culpability. This paradox has fueled debates among legal experts and philosophers, questioning how such cases should be addressed.

Lessons for the Future

The Besa Mafia case also highlighted the need to educate the public about the risks of the Dark Web. Many people view this hidden part of the internet as a lawless land, but the case showed that anonymity is never absolute and that even the darkest platforms can be exposed.

Law enforcement agencies have learned valuable lessons, developing advanced techniques to monitor the Dark Web and trace its activities. Additionally, the

case underscored the importance of international collaboration in tackling crimes that cross geographical borders.

Impact on the Perception of the Dark Web

Besa Mafia helped dispel some myths about the Dark Web. While it is a place where real crimes occur, it is also populated by scammers ready to exploit others' naivety and desperation. This dual reality has made the Dark Web an even more complex subject for the public to understand.

For many, the case served as a warning about the dangers of trusting anonymous platforms. For others, it was further confirmation that the Dark Web is a place where crime knows no borders—but neither does justice.

Conclusion: A Universal Lesson

The Besa Mafia case is not just a story of fraud but also a reflection on what

humanity is willing to do, for better or worse, when it believes it is not being watched. It showed how technology, when misused, can amplify the darkest sides of human nature. But it also demonstrated that justice can prevail, even in the darkest corners of the internet.

The Young Calabrian Hacker

A Digital Enigma

It was an ordinary morning when a high-profile Italian magistrate received an unexpected notification on his device. Seemingly harmless, the message turned out to be a chilling clue: his data had been compromised. Within minutes, his office's cybersecurity system detected suspicious activity. Someone was accessing his personal files, examining confidential information with the precision of a skilled hacker.

The magistrate in question was Nicola Gratteri, a key figure in the fight against the 'Ndrangheta, known for his relentless commitment and courage in exposing the ties between organized crime and institutions. The discovery that he was being spied upon immediately raised alarms: who could be

bold enough to violate the privacy of one of Italy's most protected figures? And what was their purpose?

This case, which would soon involve cybersecurity experts and Italian law enforcement, brought to light a young Calabrian hacker—a figure as brilliant as he was enigmatic. His involvement with the Dark Web and his advanced technical skills made him one of the most discussed actors in one of Italy's most unsettling episodes of digital espionage.

A New Kind of Threat

The Dark Web is often associated with crimes like drug trafficking, smuggling, and even murder-for-hire. However, the case of the young Calabrian hacker showed that this dark corner of the internet could also be used for subtler but equally dangerous threats: the theft and misuse of sensitive information.

With a global network of technological tools and a mind as sharp as a razor, the hacker was able to bypass even the most sophisticated security measures. His ability to remain anonymous and use the Dark Web to cover his tracks raised new concerns among Italian institutions, highlighting a level of vulnerability few were willing to admit.

As authorities began their investigation, the main question lingered: what was this young hacker's purpose? Was he acting on behalf of a larger organization? Was he driven by ideals or personal interests? The answers to these questions would reveal much more than anyone expected.

The Profile of a Digital Genius

The young Calabrian hacker at the center of one of Italy's most unsettling digital espionage episodes was no ordinary criminal. Born and raised in a small town in Calabria, he displayed an extraordinary

talent for technology from an early age. By the age of 10, he could disassemble and reassemble computers, program simple software, and navigate the web with a dexterity that astonished the adults around him.

His passion for technology grew alongside his ability to bypass security systems. During his teenage years, he became interested in hacking, drawn by the challenge of breaching seemingly impenetrable digital barriers. In an environment lacking economic and professional opportunities, the Dark Web became a space for exploration and, eventually, opportunity.

Education and Skill Development

Despite his modest background, the hacker gained access to advanced technological resources through a combination of self-teaching and online connections. Hours spent studying tutorials, manuals, and

technical documents allowed him to acquire skills rivaling those of professional experts. He specialized in penetration testing, cryptography, and digital anonymity, building a reputation as one of the best in his "field" on the Dark Web.

His psychological profile was as intriguing as his technical skills. Described by those who knew him as reserved and introverted, he was nevertheless driven by a strong determination and a desire to prove his worth. Some suggested he was motivated by a sense of rebellion against the system; others believed he was simply seeking an escape from the monotony of daily life.

A Genius in the Service of Crime?

The motivations that led him to spy on magistrates and institutions remain a matter of debate. Some suggested he was working on behalf of a criminal organization, possibly the 'Ndrangheta itself, interested in obtaining sensitive

information to protect its interests. Others believed he acted independently, aiming to sell the gathered information to the highest bidder.

Regardless of his motives, one thing was clear: his actions were the result of a brilliant mind capable of planning and executing attacks with precision that left investigators with few clues. This mix of technical genius and ambiguous morality made him an enigmatic and controversial figure.

The Espionage Techniques

The young Calabrian hacker's success in infiltrating the IT systems of Italian institutions can be attributed to a combination of advanced skills, sophisticated tools, and a deep understanding of digital vulnerabilities. His espionage techniques, though illegal, demonstrated remarkable ingenuity and

adaptability, making him a formidable adversary.

Use of Custom Malware

One of the hacker's primary tools was malware, malicious software specifically designed to compromise his victims' systems. These were custom-made programs, crafted to evade traditional antivirus software and infiltrate target devices undetected. Once installed, the malware allowed the hacker to access sensitive data, record keystrokes (keylogging), activate microphones and webcams, and even transfer files without leaving obvious traces.

Targeted Phishing Attacks

To compromise his victims, the hacker extensively used targeted phishing attacks. These attacks involved sending emails or messages that appeared to

originate from trusted sources, such as colleagues or government organizations. The messages contained links or attachments that, once clicked or opened, installed malware on the victims' devices. His emails were highly convincing, often personalized with details gathered beforehand to make the attack even more credible.

Exploitation of Zero-Day Vulnerabilities

Another key element of his arsenal was the exploitation of zero-day vulnerabilities, flaws in software or operating systems that were unknown to the manufacturers and had not yet been patched. These vulnerabilities allowed him to bypass even the most advanced system defenses, gaining privileged access without triggering any alarms. The hacker had an uncanny ability to identify these weaknesses and exploit them before they became publicly known.

Anonymous Networks and Cryptocurrencies

To cover his tracks, the young hacker used tools to ensure online anonymity, such as the Tor browser and VPN networks. These tools allowed him to mask his location and prevent his activities from being traced. Additionally, he used cryptocurrencies like Bitcoin to make transactions without leaving a clear financial trail.

The Dark Web as a Resource

The Dark Web was not just a hiding place but also a resource for obtaining tools and information. The hacker purchased exploits, malware, and other tools directly from specialized forums. He also actively participated in these communities, exchanging knowledge with other hackers and continually improving his skills.

Target Analysis

Before launching an attack, the hacker conducted meticulous analysis of his targets. He used open-source intelligence (OSINT) techniques to gather publicly available information about magistrates, such as email addresses, work habits, and social routines. This data was then combined with his technical expertise to craft highly personalized attacks.

Precision of the Attacks

A hallmark of his operations was precision. Each attack was carefully planned to avoid drawing unwanted attention. System breaches were brief and targeted, sufficient to collect the necessary information without leaving significant traces. This precision allowed him to operate for months before being discovered.

The Target: Magistrates and Institutions

One of the most unsettling aspects of the young Calabrian hacker's operations was his choice of targets: high-profile magistrates and key figures within Italian institutions. These individuals were not merely professionals but symbols of the fight against organized crime and corruption. Their exposure made the entire judicial system vulnerable to manipulation and blackmail.

Magistrates Under Attack

Among the figures targeted was Nicola Gratteri, a magistrate renowned for his battle against the 'Ndrangheta. Gratteri, an internationally respected figure, had earned a reputation for his tenacity and courage. The decision to target someone so prominent suggested that the hacker's actions were far from random: his attacks were strategically planned.

Other magistrates, less well-known but equally committed to combating crime, were also targeted. Their personal and professional communications were compromised, exposing them to potential threats and blackmail. The stolen data included emails, confidential documents, and even details about their private lives, a particularly troubling aspect that highlighted the invasive intent of the attacks.

The Risk to Institutions

Targeting magistrates was not just a personal attack but a broader threat to Italian institutions. Compromising key figures like Gratteri potentially endangered the entire judicial system. The hacker's ability to access sensitive information raised serious questions about the security of state-managed data.

In addition to magistrates, some public institutions were also targeted. IT systems in courts and government offices were probed for vulnerabilities. While many attacks were unsuccessful, the attempts themselves underscored the gravity of the situation.

Why These Targets?

The hacker's motivations for choosing magistrates and institutions as targets remain ambiguous. Some speculate that he was working on behalf of criminal organizations, which could have used the information to sabotage investigations or intimidate magistrates. Others believe he acted independently, driven by curiosity or a desire to prove his technical superiority.

Another plausible motive was profit. Selling confidential information to organizations or individuals represented a

potential incentive. The Dark Web offers numerous marketplaces where such data can fetch a high price.

The Impact of the Attacks

The attacks not only created panic among the targeted magistrates but also exposed systemic flaws in the cybersecurity of Italian institutions. The realization that a single individual could infiltrate protected networks and access sensitive data prompted a reevaluation of security measures and greater collaboration between law enforcement and cybersecurity experts.

The Investigations and the Arrest

The arrest of the young Calabrian hacker was the culmination of a complex investigation involving various cybersecurity agencies and Italian law enforcement. The operation demonstrated how sophisticated investigative techniques

were required to expose a highly skilled digital criminal.

The Start of the Investigation

The investigation began when anomalies were detected in the IT systems of magistrates and public institutions. Unauthorized access, altered files, and unusual data traffic led IT technicians to report a potential attack. The full gravity of the situation emerged when it was discovered that high-profile figures like Nicola Gratteri were among the targets.

Investigators, led by the Postal Police, began collecting digital evidence. The analysis of system logs and traces left by the attacks revealed a common pattern: the use of highly customized malware and advanced anonymity techniques.

International Collaboration

Since the Dark Web plays a crucial role in masking hackers' identities, Italian authorities collaborated with international agencies such as Europol and Interpol. Through joint efforts, they monitored Dark Web forums and cryptocurrency transactions linked to the attacks. These efforts helped trace a digital trail leading to a specific geographic location in Calabria.

Digital Tracking

Despite using tools to ensure anonymity, the hacker made several technical errors that proved crucial to the investigation. One such mistake was using an unmasked IP address during an online session. This small slip allowed investigators to identify an access point that led to a residential area.

Simultaneously, the analysis of Bitcoin transactions linked certain suspicious operations to a wallet associated with a local device. These data points, combined with traces left in compromised server logs, allowed investigators to narrow their focus on the suspect.

The Arrest Operation

The arrest was meticulously planned to ensure that all evidence was legally gathered and admissible in court. Postal Police agents raided the suspect's residence in the early morning, seizing computers, hard drives, and other electronic devices.

Among the materials collected were the malware used in the attacks, a detailed list of targets, and conversations demonstrating the deliberate intent to compromise key figures within Italian institutions. The operation ended with the

arrest of the young hacker, who was charged with unauthorized access to IT systems, digital espionage, and privacy violations.

The Impact of the Investigation

The arrest was a significant victory for law enforcement but also highlighted how vulnerable institutions could be to digital threats. The case led to a review of cybersecurity policies and the formation of new specialized teams to prevent future attacks. Additionally, it underscored the need for greater investment in monitoring and defense technologies.

Lessons and Reflections

The case of the young Calabrian hacker is not just a story of digital crimes and espionage but also a warning for institutions, companies, and individuals on how to address the threats of the digital world. His actions, though illegal,

highlighted systemic vulnerabilities and the need for a cultural shift in the perception of cybersecurity.

Lessons for Institutions

Italian institutions, and others globally, learned the importance of strengthening digital security measures. The hacker's ability to exploit vulnerabilities in government systems underscored the necessity of investing in advanced technologies and training for personnel. The case led to the creation of new cybersecurity units and greater collaboration with private sector experts to prevent future threats.

Another critical takeaway was the recognition of the need to continuously update defense systems. The hacker's use of zero-day vulnerabilities demonstrated how crucial it is to stay ahead of emerging technologies and adopt proactive strategies to mitigate risks.

Moral and Social Reflections

The hacker's profile raised broader questions about the nature of digital crime. He was a young individual with extraordinary intelligence, capable of impressive technical feats, but he chose to use his skills for illicit purposes. This sparks an ethical debate: how can society identify and support such talents, channeling them toward positive goals?

The story also highlights the importance of educating younger generations about the responsible use of technology. Access to computer knowledge is an incredible opportunity, but without moral guidance, it can become a dangerous weapon.

A Safer Future

The case of the young Calabrian hacker had a lasting impact. It pushed institutions to strengthen their defenses but also raised

public awareness about the dangers of the digital world. Protecting personal data and adopting adequate security measures have become priorities not just for organizations but also for ordinary citizens.

This story serves as a warning: technological progress is a double-edged sword. For every innovation that enhances our lives, there is potential for abuse that threatens our security. The key is to remain vigilant, collaborate, and invest in a safer digital future.

The Dark Web Network of Date Rape Drugs

An Invisible Substance, a Silent Crime

It was an ordinary evening in a quiet Italian town when a young woman began to feel strangely disoriented. Her drink, seemingly harmless, concealed an invisible threat: a dose of GHB, commonly known as the "date rape drug." Before she could understand what was happening, the substance had already taken effect, leaving her vulnerable and unable to resist.

This type of crime, insidious and devastating, is sadly made even easier by the Dark Web, a hidden network where anonymity and impunity allow the trade of illegal substances like GHB, Rohypnol, and other sedative drugs. In 2022, an extensive investigation in Italy uncovered a criminal network using the Dark Web to traffic these

substances. The operation resulted in 39 arrests, but not before their actions caused irreparable harm to numerous victims.

A Growing Dark Market

Date rape drugs are not new, but their availability through the Dark Web has amplified the problem. These substances, odorless and tasteless, are often used to incapacitate victims for sexual assaults or robberies. The anonymity provided by Dark Web platforms and the use of cryptocurrencies like Bitcoin have made the trafficking of these substances extremely difficult to track and combat.

Every purchase on the Dark Web contributes to a complex system where manufacturers, distributors, and buyers work together to circumvent the law. This is not just an Italian problem; the trade of these substances is a global phenomenon, with

roots extending to multiple countries and international criminal networks.

A Silent Crime

What makes these drugs particularly insidious is the difficulty in detecting them. Often administered without the victim's knowledge, their effects wear off quickly, leaving little evidence for investigators. This creates a vicious cycle of fear and silence, where many victims choose not to report the abuse out of shame or lack of proof.

The operation that dismantled this network of traffickers was not only a victory for Italian law enforcement but also an example of how technology can be used to fight crime. However, it raised pressing questions: how many similar networks exist? And what measures can be taken to protect people from these crimes?

How the Network Operated

The success of the date rape drug trafficking network dismantled in Italy was tied to a well-organized system that exploited the Dark Web's capabilities. Anonymity, cryptocurrencies, and illegal trade platforms created a fertile environment for buying and selling dangerous substances like GHB, Rohypnol, and other benzodiazepines.

Production and Sourcing

Date rape drugs were primarily produced in clandestine laboratories, both within and outside Italy. Some of the most sought-after substances were imported from countries with less stringent pharmaceutical regulations. Producers used the Dark Web to connect with suppliers of chemical raw materials, ordering specific compounds that were difficult to trace.

In some cases, the trafficking relied on legitimate drugs that were stolen or

obtained through falsified prescriptions, which were then manipulated to create more concentrated and lethal versions. These products were packaged to appear harmless, such as bottles of dietary supplements or essential oils, to evade postal inspections.

Dark Web Sales Platforms

The platforms used for selling date rape drugs operated much like traditional e-commerce marketplaces. Users could browse detailed catalogs, read reviews left by other buyers, and select the desired product. Every transaction was conducted in cryptocurrency, predominantly Bitcoin or Monero, to ensure the anonymity of both the seller and the buyer.

These markets also offered an escrow system, where buyers' funds were held until the product was delivered. This helped build trust among users, further incentivizing illegal trade.

Distribution and Logistics

Once the transaction was complete, the distribution of substances was carried out using ingenious methods to avoid detection. Traffickers used anonymous shipping and sophisticated concealment techniques, such as packaging within common items or using fake addresses.

Packages were shipped via international postal services or private couriers, often with labels indicating innocuous contents. In some cases, traffickers arranged local deliveries through intermediaries, further reducing the risk of direct exposure.

Buyers and Motivations

Buyers of these substances included a wide range of individuals: criminals intending to use the drugs to commit sexual assaults, ordinary people drawn to experimenting with illegal substances, and even college students unaware of the risks.

The ease of accessing these platforms, combined with the perception of anonymity, created a false sense of security for many buyers. However, purchasing these drugs often led to devastating consequences for both victims and consumers.

The Role of the Dark Web

The Dark Web was the beating heart of this network, providing the infrastructure necessary to connect sellers and buyers worldwide. The lack of regulation and the difficulty in monitoring criminal activities made these platforms particularly challenging to dismantle.

Investigative Techniques

Dismantling the date rape drug trafficking network represented one of the most complex operations ever conducted by Italian law enforcement. The success of this mission relied on a combination of advanced

investigative techniques, international collaborations, and cutting-edge technology.

Dark Web Monitoring

Investigators began by tracking activities on specific Dark Web platforms known for trading illegal substances. This process required weeks of work, during which agents analyzed hundreds of sales listings, buyer reviews, and cryptocurrency transactions. Using specialized software, they were able to map interactions between users and identify suspicious behavior patterns.

Cryptocurrency Tracking

A key element of the investigation was monitoring transactions in Bitcoin and Monero, the cryptocurrencies most commonly used for payments on the Dark Web. Although these currencies provide a level of anonymity, investigators exploited wallet

and exchange platform vulnerabilities to trace money flows. By cross-referencing this information with purchase and shipping data, they were able to link multiple sellers and buyers.

Undercover Agents

One of the most effective tools was the infiltration of undercover agents into Dark Web communities. Posing as interested buyers, agents established direct contacts with sellers, negotiating substance purchases and obtaining critical information about distribution methods. In some cases, they even identified intermediaries responsible for shipments.

Digital Forensic Analysis

The seizure of servers and electronic devices during the investigation allowed cybersecurity experts to analyze vast amounts of data. Through data mining and

forensic analysis, conversations, documents, and transaction histories were recovered, directly linking suspects to the date rape drug trade.

International Collaboration

Since the trafficking network extended beyond Italian borders, authorities collaborated with Europol and Interpol, as well as agencies from countries such as the United States and Germany. This collaboration enabled real-time information sharing, the localization of international sellers, and the coordination of simultaneous raids in multiple nations.

The Role of Advanced Technology

The use of artificial intelligence and machine learning algorithms was crucial in identifying behavior patterns within the collected data. These tools helped

investigators predict suspects' moves, anticipate their evasion strategies, and ultimately dismantle the entire network.

The Final Operation and Arrests

The culminating operation that dismantled the date rape drug trafficking network was one of the most significant interventions by Italian law enforcement against Dark Web-related crime. After months of meticulous investigations, authorities coordinated a large-scale operation that led to the arrest of 39 individuals across various regions of Italy.

Operation Preparation

The final phase of the investigation was planned with extreme precision. Investigators gathered sufficient evidence to secure search and arrest warrants while simultaneously monitoring the movements of key suspects. Through collaboration with

Europol and Interpol, authorities were able to trace the geographical locations of several key members of the network, including producers and distributors.

Information collected during the preceding months was used to establish strategic intervention points, ensuring that no suspect could escape. Specialized cybersecurity agents and tactical teams were deployed to conduct simultaneous raids in multiple locations.

The Day of the Operation

At dawn, in a series of coordinated raids, law enforcement stormed homes, clandestine laboratories, and warehouses used for storing the substances. Agents seized computers, servers, cryptocurrencies, and large quantities of drugs, including GHB and Rohypnol, packaged in ways that facilitated anonymous distribution.

Among the recovered materials were detailed buyer lists, Dark Web transaction logs, and

documentation highlighting the international scope of the network. The operation concluded with the arrest of 39 individuals, charged with production, trafficking, and sale of illegal substances, as well as conspiracy.

Cryptocurrency Seizure

A critical aspect of the operation was the seizure of digital wallets containing cryptocurrencies valued at over one million euros. This dealt a significant blow to the network, as the confiscated funds were intended for reinvestment in raw materials and logistical operations.

Investigators worked with blockchain experts to further trace the funds, aiming to identify potential international accomplices and dismantle additional operational cells.

Operation Outcomes

The operation was a success not only in terms of arrests but also in its impact on the illegal market for date rape drugs. The dismantling of this network led to a temporary decrease in the availability of these substances on the Dark Web, giving authorities a crucial advantage in strengthening preventive measures.

The information collected during the raids provided new leads for further investigations, suggesting that this network was only one of many active in the trafficking of illegal substances via the Dark Web.

The Trial and Consequences

The trial following the operation against the date rape drug trafficking network was a pivotal moment for the Italian justice system, shedding light on both the scale of the crime and the challenges of prosecuting digital offenses. The 39 individuals

arrested faced serious charges, including international trafficking of illegal substances, conspiracy, and money laundering through cryptocurrencies.

The Charges and the Trial

The defendants were brought before a special tribunal equipped with experts in cybercrime and transnational offenses. During the trial, the prosecution presented overwhelming evidence: intercepted communications on the Dark Web, Bitcoin transactions, and records directly linking the suspects to criminal activities. Testimonies from undercover agents played a crucial role, providing insights into the network's inner workings and the techniques used to avoid detection.

Defense lawyers attempted to challenge the validity of digital evidence, arguing that some transactions could have been made by other individuals using falsified identities. However, the meticulous

collection and analysis of evidence by investigators made it difficult to sustain such claims.

The Sentences

The trial concluded with exemplary sentences for most defendants. Several network leaders received prison terms exceeding 20 years, while intermediaries and distributors were sentenced to between 5 and 15 years. Financial penalties included the seizure of assets and cryptocurrencies used to fund operations.

The convictions sent a strong message to the criminal community: not even the anonymity of the Dark Web is sufficient to evade justice. This outcome was positively received by both institutions and the public, who saw the operation as an example of how technology can be harnessed to combat crime.

Impact on Victims

A critical aspect highlighted during the trial was the devastating impact of these drugs on victims. Heart-wrenching testimonies revealed the pain and trauma suffered by those exposed to these substances. Some victims recounted difficulties in reporting abuses due to shame and lack of evidence, emphasizing the need for greater public awareness and support systems.

The trial also led to the introduction of new initiatives aimed at protecting victims, such as educational campaigns and increased investment in technology to detect these substances in drinks. These steps were considered essential to prevent future abuses and provide victims with a path to healing.

Long-Term Consequences

The operation and trial had a lasting impact on the trafficking of drugs via the Dark Web. Many illegal marketplaces temporarily shut down, fearing detection, and some platforms implemented stricter measures to monitor suspicious activities.

From a legislative perspective, the case prompted Italian authorities to strengthen laws against digital crimes, introducing harsher penalties and incentives for tech companies to cooperate with law enforcement. Additionally, it inspired greater international collaboration to address the challenges posed by digital crime.

Lessons and Impact on Security

The case of the date rape drug trafficking network left a profound impact not only on law enforcement but also on public opinion

and institutions. This episode highlighted the challenges of digital security, the role of the Dark Web in transnational crimes, and the need for greater public awareness.

Lessons for the Future

The case demonstrated the importance of investing in advanced technologies to combat digital crimes. The use of artificial intelligence, blockchain, and advanced analytics tools enabled investigators to dismantle a complex and well-organized network. However, it remains clear that digital crime evolves rapidly, and authorities must stay one step ahead.

Another key lesson concerns international collaboration. Without the support of Europol, Interpol, and other foreign agencies, it would have been impossible to target a network with global ramifications. This underscores the need to strengthen

ties between nations to address shared threats.

The Role of Public Education

One of the most critical areas highlighted was the need to educate the public about the dangers of date rape drugs and the workings of the Dark Web. Awareness campaigns can help prevent future crimes by increasing potential victims' understanding and encouraging safer behaviors.

Additionally, digital education should be integrated into school curricula to prepare new generations to understand the risks and opportunities of the online world. Understanding how anonymous platforms and cryptocurrency methods work can be a tool to reduce the misuse of technologies.

Toward Better Digital Security

Institutions have realized that fighting digital crime requires significant resources and ongoing commitment. Following the operation, Italy began developing new protocols to monitor suspicious activities on the Dark Web and strengthen laws against digital crimes.

Globally, the case contributed to a broader dialogue on cryptocurrency regulation and the need for better tools to track illicit transactions. While the Dark Web remains a place of great anonymity, this episode showed that no criminal is truly safe.

A Message for the Future

The case of the date rape drug network reminds us that technology is a double-edged sword. It can be used to improve people's lives but also to perpetrate acts of violence and abuse. The key to the

future is to remain vigilant, collaborate internationally, and continue innovating to protect everyone's safety.

Red Rooms

Reality or Myth of the Dark Web?

It was a dark and silent night when an anonymous user on a Dark Web forum posted a cryptic message: "Live stream. A red room. The horror begins at 11 PM. Payment only in Bitcoin." This deliberately vague and chilling description immediately ignited the imagination of anyone who read it. Was it just a marketing ploy? Or did it truly hide a real horror?

Red Rooms are a recurring element in the darkest tales linked to the Dark Web. According to legend, these rooms are digital spaces where anonymous viewers can pay to watch live streams of torture or murder.

But how much truth is there to these stories? And what makes Red Rooms such a persistent legend?

The Origin and Spread of the Myth

Stories about Red Rooms began circulating in the early 2000s, fueled by the growing notoriety of the Dark Web as a hub for illegal activities and extreme content. Films, creepypasta, and dedicated forums helped create an aura of mystery around these alleged live broadcasts.

A significant contribution to the myth of Red Rooms came with the spread of shock videos, often fake, that claimed to depict scenes of extreme violence. These contents, though frequently debunked as edits or viral campaigns, reinforced the belief that corners of the Dark Web exist where horror knows no limits.

The Collective Imagination

Red Rooms embody some of humanity's deepest fears: the anonymity that allows evil to thrive, the loss of control, and the idea that voyeurism could turn into complicity with crime.

What makes the myth of Red Rooms particularly unsettling is its surface plausibility. In today's world, where technology allows real-time broadcasting to millions of people, it's easy to imagine someone exploiting these capabilities for malicious purposes.

A Starting Point to Uncover the Truth

This introduction raises a fundamental question: do Red Rooms truly exist, or are they a product of collective imagination influenced by sensationalist media and fear of the unknown? The following sections will delve into the origins, evidence, and controversial opinions surrounding one of the Dark Web's most persistent myths.

What Are Red Rooms?

Red Rooms are described as secret digital spaces accessible only through the Dark Web, where extreme acts of violence, torture, or murder are live-streamed for a paying audience. The idea of these digital venues has captured the imagination of many, fueled by unsettling stories, creepypasta, and media portrayals. But what exactly are Red Rooms, and why do they remain such a topic of fascination and fear?

Typical Description of Red Rooms

According to narratives, Red Rooms function as real-time streaming platforms where viewers can not only watch but also interact with the perpetrators of violent acts. Through payments in cryptocurrencies like Bitcoin or Monero, users can "buy" specific actions to be performed on the victim, turning the stream into an interactive experience.

The stories describe dark, barren rooms lit only by a sinister red light, from which the name "Red Room" derives. Victims, often bound or sedated, are placed at the center of the scene, while their tormentors follow the instructions of viewers in exchange for money.

Key Characteristics

Anonymity: Red Rooms are allegedly accessible only through the Dark Web, using tools like Tor to ensure the secrecy of the identities of both viewers and organizers.

Cryptocurrencies: Payments are exclusively made in digital currencies to make transaction tracing difficult.

Interactivity: What makes Red Rooms unique is the idea that viewers can directly influence what happens during the broadcast.

Exclusivity: Access is often described as restricted to an elite group of users with significant financial resources.

Origins of the Descriptions

Descriptions of Red Rooms stem from a mix of horror narratives, conspiracy theories, and cultural references. Films like *Hostel* and *Unfriended: Dark Web* have contributed to embedding the idea that such places could exist. Additionally, creepypasta and stories on online forums have further disseminated these tales, often without verification.

The Search for Evidence

Despite numerous claims, no concrete evidence has ever been found to prove the existence of Red Rooms. Many shock videos marketed as Red Rooms have been debunked as fake, edited footage, or viral advertising campaigns. However, the lack of evidence

has not stopped the myth from spreading, as it continues to thrive on the allure of the forbidden and the mystery surrounding the Dark Web.

Investigations and Controversies

Red Rooms are an enigma shrouded in mystery, fueled by intense public curiosity and the inability to definitively prove or disprove their existence. Authorities and cybersecurity experts have conducted numerous investigations to shed light on this Dark Web myth, often yielding more questions than definitive answers.

Official Investigations

Various governments and security agencies have addressed the topic of Red Rooms, often as part of broader operations against illegal content trafficking on the Dark Web. One of the earliest significant investigations occurred in 2015, when

Interpol launched an operation targeting distribution networks for illegal materials. During this operation, forums and platforms claiming to host Red Rooms were monitored, but no concrete evidence of their existence was found.

In Italy, law enforcement conducted similar operations, focusing on suspected criminal activities on the Dark Web. Again, despite traces of suspicious traffic and disturbing content, no actual Red Rooms were ever identified.

The Controversies

One of the most controversial aspects of Red Rooms is the use of the myth to create moral panic and fuel media clickbait. Many experts argue that the narrative of Red Rooms is largely a product of sensationalism, reinforced by unverified stories and the lack of clear regulation of the Dark Web.

Some cases of shock videos, presented as recordings of Red Rooms, were later proven to be fake or the result of editing. For instance, the infamous "Daisy's Destruction" case, often linked to Red Rooms, was actually a criminal video distributed offline and not live-streamed. This has led many to question the distinction between myth and reality in Dark Web tales.

The Limits of Investigations

Despite efforts, investigating Red Rooms presents numerous challenges. The Dark Web is designed to ensure anonymity, making it difficult for authorities to identify users, platforms, and transactions. Furthermore, many claims about Red Rooms are based on anonymous forums or unverifiable sources, complicating investigations further.

Another limitation lies in the technology required to broadcast live content on the

Dark Web. Unlike platforms like YouTube or Twitch, the Dark Web lacks reliable infrastructure for real-time streaming, making the existence of Red Rooms as described in myths logistically challenging.

Indirect Evidence and Suspicious Cases

Although definitive evidence has never been found, some suspicious cases have fueled belief in Red Rooms. For instance, in 2017, a joint operation by Europol and the FBI led to the shutdown of a site claiming to offer access to extreme live content. However, authorities found no evidence of live-streamed murders or torture.

These episodes demonstrate that while the Red Room myth may be exaggerated, the existence of extreme content on the Dark Web is an undeniable reality. However, the narrative of Red Rooms as places of interactive horror remains unconfirmed.

The Technical Aspect and Challenges

Despite the aura of mystery surrounding Red Rooms, their alleged existence clashes with several technical challenges. Broadcasting extreme content live on the Dark Web requires a level of infrastructure and technology often underestimated in sensationalist narratives.

The Complexities of Streaming on the Dark Web

The Dark Web is a part of the internet accessible only through specialized software like Tor, designed to ensure anonymity. While it is ideal for encrypted communications and anonymous transactions, it is not optimized for real-time video streaming.

Bandwidth limitations: The Tor network is not designed to handle the heavy traffic required for video streaming. Connection speeds are often slow and unstable, making

it difficult to provide smooth, continuous broadcasts.

Detectability: Even with the anonymity provided by Tor, broadcasting live video generates significant data flow that could attract the attention of authorities or cybersecurity experts.

Required infrastructure: Organizing a Red Room would require advanced setups with secure servers and customized software to avoid detection. This type of infrastructure is complex and expensive to implement.

Security and Cryptocurrencies

Cryptocurrencies like Bitcoin and Monero are often mentioned in Red Room narratives as the payment method to maintain anonymity. However, even encrypted transactions can leave traces that, with advanced tools, can be followed to some extent.

Traceable wallets: While some cryptocurrencies offer higher privacy levels, like Monero, using online wallets or centralized exchanges can create vulnerabilities.

High costs: Creating a Red Room would require a secure payment network and escrow mechanisms to avoid scams, further increasing costs for alleged organizers.

Interactivity: Myth or Reality?

A central element of Red Rooms is interactivity, meaning viewers can directly influence the actions being streamed. While compelling in horror narratives, this concept presents significant logistical challenges:

Synchronization: Ensuring real-time communication between viewers and organizers would require a stable and fast connection, something difficult to achieve on the Dark Web.

Moderation: An interactive system would need a platform capable of handling multiple requests and simultaneous payments, increasing technical complexity.

Fake scenarios: Many alleged interactive Red Rooms have turned out to be pre-recorded videos or staged acts designed to deceive viewers.

Human Factors and Exposure Risk

Even with the best technological precautions, the human element remains a critical vulnerability. Organizing a Red Room would require the involvement of multiple people, increasing the risk of errors or exposure.

Collaborators: Involving others to organize and manage a Red Room increases the likelihood of information leaks or infiltration.

Victims and investigations: Potential victims could survive and provide

testimonies, as has happened in some cases of shock videos erroneously associated with Red Rooms.

Conclusion

The technical and logistical challenges make the existence of Red Rooms, as described in myths, highly improbable. While the Dark Web hosts extreme content, the idea of a place where torture and murder are live-streamed with audience interaction seems more like a fear-fueled fantasy than a documented reality.

Reality vs Fiction

Red Rooms represent one of the most persistent myths associated with the Dark Web, but their real nature remains a subject of debate. While some argue that Red Rooms do exist, much evidence suggests they are largely a product of collective

imagination, fueled by sensationalist media and fear of the unknown.

Real Events Associated with Red Rooms

Over the years, certain events have been mistakenly linked to Red Rooms, contributing to their legend. An example is the case of "Daisy's Destruction," a horrifying video produced by a known pedophile that was initially interpreted as a Red Room. However, it was pre-recorded content distributed through criminal networks, not a live broadcast with audience interaction.

Other instances of extreme violence documented on the Dark Web are often mistaken for Red Rooms but lack key elements: interactivity and real-time transmission. This suggests that while disturbing content exists, the Red Room myth is an exaggeration.

Creepypasta and Online Narratives

Much of Red Rooms' popularity can be attributed to "creepypasta," horror stories circulated online for entertainment. Tales like "Blank Room Soup" or alleged Tor streams are often presented as truths but turn out to be fictional creations designed to scare and entertain.

Online forums dedicated to the Dark Web often amplify these tales, blending facts and fiction. The result is a narrative that seems plausible but lacks concrete evidence.

Media Perception

Mainstream media have played a crucial role in solidifying the Red Room myth. Sensationalist documentaries and articles promising to reveal the "darkest secrets of the Dark Web" often report unverified stories, perpetuating the idea that Red Rooms are real.

This distorted portrayal often serves to generate clicks and views but contributes to creating a moral panic that makes it difficult to distinguish myth from reality. Cybersecurity experts emphasize that the lack of concrete evidence is a key indicator of Red Rooms' non-existence.

The Boundary Between Myth and Reality

The line between myth and reality is often blurred, especially in the context of the Dark Web.

Real Elements: It is undeniable that violent and extreme content exists on the Dark Web, but it does not match the description of Red Rooms. Videos of torture and murder have been found in the past, but these were recordings, not live streams.

Fictional Elements: The more sensationalist aspects of Red Rooms, such as interactivity and customization of acts, appear to be the product of horror narratives rather than documented reality.

The Allure of the Myth

The Red Room myth persists because it taps into deep aspects of human psychology. Fear of the unknown, fascination with horror, and curiosity about the forbidden create fertile ground for these stories to spread. Additionally, the anonymity of the Dark Web fuels the idea that unimaginable crimes can be committed without consequences.

Conclusion

While the Red Room myth is wrapped in a fascinating and disturbing narrative, concrete evidence supporting their existence is virtually non-existent. Red Rooms seem to be a product of fear, imagination, and media sensationalism rather than documented reality. However, their cultural impact demonstrates the power of the intersection between technology and storytelling.

Psychological and Cultural Impact

Red Rooms, whether real or imagined, have had a profound impact on collective psychology and contemporary culture. Their narrative has fueled deep fears and reflections on ethics, voyeurism, and the dark potential of technology.

The Attraction to the Forbidden

The myth of Red Rooms captures attention due to its forbidden and disturbing nature. The combination of anonymity, horror, and the possibility of interaction draws morbid curiosity, even among those who morally condemn such acts. This attraction to the forbidden is not new: historically, humans have been fascinated by what is considered taboo or morally unacceptable.

Effect on Perception of the Dark Web

Red Rooms have solidified the image of the Dark Web as a place of absolute evil, where

unimaginable crimes are committed unchecked. While the Dark Web does host illegal activities and extreme content, this one-sided representation overlooks its legitimate uses, such as protecting privacy and freedom of expression.

The constant association of Red Rooms with the Dark Web has also created moral panic, pushing governments and media to focus on stricter regulations and surveillance measures rather than fostering balanced dialogue.

Ethical Implications of Voyeurism

The concept of Red Rooms raises complex ethical questions about voyeurism and complicity. Watching acts of violence, even fictional ones, fuels a debate about the line between entertainment and morality. If Red Rooms were real, viewers would be directly responsible for the atrocities committed, an extreme form of passive but culpable participation.

This debate is also reflected in mainstream media, with films and TV series exploring the theme of violent voyeurism and its psychological consequences.

Cultural Impact

Red Rooms have become a symbol of the dark potential of technology. Films, books, and video games have exploited this narrative to create stories of suspense and horror, deeply influencing popular culture.

For example, movies like *Unfriended: Dark Web* and video games inspired by Dark Web legends reflect the fascination and fear associated with these tales. These cultural products, while fictional, perpetuate the myth and embed it into collective imagination.

Consequences on Mental Health

The spread of stories about Red Rooms can have negative effects on mental health,

especially for those who are already vulnerable. Fear of becoming victims of such crimes or mere exposure to related content can cause anxiety, paranoia, and other forms of psychological distress.

Additionally, the normalization of violent narratives can desensitize people, making violence a less shocking and more accepted element in society.

Conclusion

The psychological and cultural impact of Red Rooms extends beyond the question of their existence. These stories act as a mirror to our darkest fears and desires, challenging the relationship between technology, morality, and entertainment. Regardless of their reality, Red Rooms will continue to influence how we perceive the Dark Web and the potential of digital anonymity.

Red Rooms embody an enigma of our times, a myth fueled by fear of the unknown and the

growing power of technology. While no concrete evidence exists to prove their reality, their narrative has left an indelible mark on collective imagination and perceptions of the Dark Web.

What We Have Learned

Through exploring the phenomenon of Red Rooms, several fundamental truths emerge:

The Power of Narratives: Red Rooms are a striking example of how well-crafted stories can profoundly influence culture and collective thought, regardless of their truth.

The Role of the Dark Web: While often associated with crime and extreme content, the Dark Web is also a tool for free expression and privacy protection.

The Impact of Fear: The Red Room myth demonstrates how fear of the unknown can create moral panic and lead to disproportionate reactions, such as overly

strict regulations or sensationalist media campaigns.

A Message for the Future

Red Rooms, real or not, remind us of the power and dangers of technology. As a society, we must address the ethical and moral implications of digitization and anonymity, striking a balance between innovation and security.

Human curiosity about the dark is natural, but it is essential to distinguish myth from reality to prevent unfounded fears from negatively shaping our way of life and interaction with technology.

The Myth That Persists

Despite the lack of evidence, it is unlikely that the Red Room myth will disappear. Its persistence is a testament to our fascination with horror and the unexplored boundaries of the web. And

perhaps, in some way, Red Rooms will continue to exist, not as a tangible reality but as a metaphor for our deepest fears and the darkest potential of the digital world.

Welcome to Video: The Largest Archive of Digital Terror

Introduction: A Global Archive of Horrors

In 2019, the digital world was shaken by the discovery of a platform that had amassed an unprecedented volume of illegal content related to the sexual exploitation of minors. "Welcome to Video" was not just a site hidden within the Dark Web; it represented a global network of criminals exchanging horrifying content with unparalleled ease. The platform, which exclusively accepted Bitcoin payments, had built a simple and accessible system for distributing child exploitation videos, attracting users from every corner of the globe.

This network of horrors not only exploited advanced technologies to ensure anonymity and protection for its users but did so with terrifying efficiency. The discovery of "Welcome to Video" led to an international investigation involving more than 300 individuals across 38 countries, marking a pivotal moment in the fight against online crimes. The platform was not merely a site for exchange but a criminal ecosystem designed to incentivize and normalize some of the most heinous abuses.

As the site was dismantled and its operators arrested, shocking details emerged about the scale of its operations and the devastating impact on its victims. While the case represented a significant victory for law enforcement, it also exposed glaring gaps in combating such crimes and the urgent need for increasingly sophisticated tools to fight digital criminal networks.

This is the story of "Welcome to Video": a case that exposed the darkest side of

technology and prompted the world to reflect on the urgency of protecting the most vulnerable in an increasingly connected era.

How Welcome to Video Operated

A System Built on Anonymity

Welcome to Video was designed to maximize the anonymity and security features offered by the Dark Web. The platform utilized the Tor network, ensuring that both users and administrators could operate without being tracked. This system, combined with the exclusive use of cryptocurrencies, made Welcome to Video one of the most advanced and difficult-to-detect sites of its kind.

Access and Registration: Accessing the platform required the installation of the Tor browser. Users could register with anonymous email addresses and pseudonyms, ensuring maximum discretion. Once registered, they had access to thousands of videos organized into categories.

Bitcoin Payments: To download content, users had to make payments in Bitcoin. This system not only incentivized the use of cryptocurrencies but also created a barrier of entry, ensuring that only serious and motivated users participated.

Incentives for Sharing: Welcome to Video encouraged users to upload new content in exchange for free credits on the platform. This model promoted a constant expansion of the archive of illegal material, making it an active node in the distribution of child exploitation videos.

Simple Interface: Unlike other Dark Web platforms, Welcome to Video was surprisingly user-friendly. Its interface resembled that of a common streaming site, with search functions, playlists, and automatic suggestions. This level of accessibility made it attractive to a wide range of users.

A Global Network of Horror

Welcome to Video was not limited to a single country or region. The platform boasted users from around the world, with a high concentration in countries such as the United States, the United Kingdom, South Korea, and Germany. Its global popularity stemmed from its simplicity and effectiveness in providing illegal content without compromising user anonymity.

User Collaboration: Users often shared information on how to remain anonymous, evade authorities, and safely exchange Bitcoin.

Local Content Production: In some cases, users themselves produced videos, actively contributing to the platform's archive.

The Illusion of Security

Despite its technological sophistication, Welcome to Video was not flawless. The administrators made critical mistakes that

ultimately led to their exposure. Mismanagement of Bitcoin payments, combined with the use of unprotected IP addresses in certain operations, allowed authorities to trace transactions and identify both the administrators and many users of the platform.

This case demonstrated that, while the Dark Web may offer an ostensibly impenetrable level of anonymity, the combination of advanced technology and international cooperation can break even the most secure networks.

Victims: Unimaginable Harm

The Horror Behind Each Video

Behind every video uploaded to Welcome to Video lay a story of suffering, fear, and trauma. The victims, often children aged between 3 and 12, came from diverse backgrounds but shared a common fate: being exploited and abused to fuel a global criminal network.

How Victims Were Targeted

Welcome to Video users employed various strategies to locate and groom victims. Often, the content uploaded was produced by members of the platform themselves or by local abuse networks.

Online Grooming: Social media platforms and messaging apps were favored by predators to target vulnerable children. By posing as peers or using fake identities, they built trust, which was then exploited to obtain images and videos.

Domestic Exploitation: In some cases, abusers were family members or individuals close to the victims who produced content to sell or share on the platform.

Trafficking of Pre-Existing Material: Welcome to Video also served as an archive for videos already in circulation on the Dark Web, perpetuating the exploitation of past abuse victims.

Psychological Impact on Victims

The abuse suffered by Welcome to Video victims had devastating consequences, with long-term effects that often lasted a lifetime.

Post-Traumatic Stress Disorder (PTSD): Victims experienced recurring nightmares, flashbacks, and panic attacks related to the abuse.

Anxiety and Depression: Many children developed emotional disorders that hindered their ability to interact with others and lead normal lives.

Shame and Isolation: Feelings of guilt and fear of judgment often prevented victims from speaking out, hindering their path to recovery.

A System That Incentivized Abuse

Welcome to Video did not merely distribute illegal content; it actively incentivized the production of new videos. Users earned

credits for uploading material, creating a perverse cycle that increased the number of victims involved.

Growing Demand for Content: The availability of increasingly extreme material pushed predators to produce more degrading and violent videos.

Normalization of Abuse: The online community provided a platform where users supported each other, justifying their crimes as acceptable.

The Redemption of Victims

The operation that dismantled Welcome to Video led to the identification and rescue of dozens of victims. For many of them, the path to healing remains long, but the psychological support and resources provided by authorities and non-profit organizations represent an essential first step.

This case highlights the need for greater awareness and prevention tools to protect children, the most vulnerable victims of the digital world.

Investigations and International Cooperation

A Global Operation

The investigation into Welcome to Video represents one of the most significant international efforts ever undertaken against online crime. The case began when South Korean authorities discovered the platform during an investigation into child exploitation content. Hosted on South Korean servers, the site was the hub of a global network of users. However, the real breakthrough came with the use of advanced technologies to trace Bitcoin transactions.

The Role of Cryptocurrencies

Welcome to Video exclusively accepted Bitcoin as a payment method, providing its users with an illusion of anonymity. This technological choice, initially considered an advantage by the administrators, ultimately proved to be a critical vulnerability.

Blockchain Analysis: Authorities leveraged the public nature of Bitcoin transactions to trace the flow of funds to cryptocurrency exchanges.

Human Errors: Some users and administrators failed to use sufficiently sophisticated techniques to protect their identities, allowing law enforcement to link Bitcoin addresses to real names.

Collaboration with Exchanges: Cryptocurrency exchanges played a key role in identifying users, providing information on accounts linked to suspicious transactions.

International Cooperation

The global reach of the platform necessitated close collaboration among law enforcement agencies from multiple countries. In addition to South Korea, which led the operation, agencies such as Europol, the FBI, and UK authorities were involved.

Information Sharing: Agencies coordinated their efforts through international databases, exchanging evidence and details about identified users.

Simultaneous Arrests: The operation culminated in a series of synchronized arrests across 38 countries, with the seizure of servers, devices, and vast amounts of illegal material.

Victim Support: During the investigations, dozens of victims were identified, many of whom were rescued from ongoing abuse.

The Fall of the Primary Administrator

The founder and chief administrator of Welcome to Video, a South Korean citizen named Jong Woo Son, was identified and arrested by local authorities. During the trial, disturbing details emerged about his management of the platform and the scale of the material hosted. Son was sentenced to 18 months in prison in South Korea, with additional charges awaiting him in the United States.

A Landmark Case

The investigation into Welcome to Video not only led to the closure of one of the most prolific platforms on the Dark Web but also set a new standard for international cooperation and the use of technology in investigations. This case demonstrated that, even in the seemingly anonymous world of the Dark Web, mistakes and vulnerabilities can be exploited to ensure justice.

The Dismantling and Legal Consequences

The Shutdown of Welcome to Video

The dismantling of Welcome to Video stands as one of the most significant operations in the fight against online sexual exploitation. After years of coordinated investigations, law enforcement agencies successfully dismantled the platform, seizing its servers and arresting hundreds of users worldwide. This achievement was made possible through a combination of advanced investigative techniques and international collaboration.

Server Seizures: South Korean authorities, supported by international agencies, located and seized the primary servers hosting the site. The servers contained terabytes of illegal material, unveiling the full scale of the platform's operations.

Global Arrests: Over 300 individuals were arrested across 38 countries, including

administrators, collaborators, and active users of the platform.

Victim Rescues: During the operation, dozens of victims were identified and rescued, many of whom were still trapped in abusive situations.

Legal Consequences

The arrests led to a series of trials in multiple countries, with charges ranging from the production and distribution of child exploitation material to money laundering.

Severe Sentences: Many defendants received harsh sentences, with penalties ranging from 10 years to life imprisonment.

Asset Forfeitures: Authorities seized millions of dollars in Bitcoin and other cryptocurrencies, representing the illegal profits generated through the platform's transactions.

Victim Support Collaboration: Non-profit organizations and local governments worked to provide psychological and legal support to the identified victims.

Changes in Laws and Policies

The Welcome to Video case had a profound impact not only on judicial outcomes but also on the formulation of new laws and policies to combat online crimes.

New Cryptocurrency Regulations: Many countries introduced stricter laws to monitor Bitcoin and cryptocurrency transactions, making anonymity more difficult.

Enhanced International Collaboration: The operation's success highlighted the importance of global cooperation, prompting nations to strengthen communication channels among agencies.

Awareness Campaigns: Governments and non-profits launched initiatives to educate the

public about the dangers of the Dark Web and to encourage reporting of suspicious activities.

A Warning for the Future

The dismantling of Welcome to Video was a pivotal step in the fight against online sexual exploitation, but it also underscored the resilience of criminal networks. New platforms continue to emerge, demonstrating that the battle against these crimes is far from over. This case serves as a reminder of the power of technology and the need to use it responsibly to protect the most vulnerable.

Conclusion: A Victory in the Fight Against Online Crime

The Welcome to Video case marked a milestone in the battle against online sexual exploitation, demonstrating how technology can be both a double-edged sword

and a tool for justice. The platform's dismantling exposed the global scale of the issue and underscored the importance of coordinated international action.

This operation was not only an investigative success but also a reminder of the immense work still required. Every platform shut down represents a victory, yet new networks continue to emerge, quickly adapting to enforcement efforts.

A Message of Hope and Responsibility

The story of Welcome to Video highlights that, despite the complexity of the challenges, determination and international collaboration can lead to significant outcomes. Every victim rescued and every criminal apprehended is a step forward toward a safer digital world.

However, it is crucial for governments, tech companies, and ordinary citizens to work together to prevent and combat these crimes. Education and awareness remain key

tools in protecting the most vulnerable and creating a safer global network.

Welcome to Video is not only a dark chapter in the history of the web but also a testament to human resilience and the ability to make a difference in the face of adversity.

AlphaBay: The Supermarket of Digital Crime

Introduction: The Rise of AlphaBay

Between 2014 and 2017, AlphaBay established itself as the largest black market on the Dark Web, surpassing even the legendary Silk Road in size and scope. Dubbed the "supermarket of digital crime," AlphaBay offered an extensive range of illegal goods and services, including drugs, weapons, stolen data, forged documents, and hacking tools. With millions of users worldwide and daily transactions totaling millions of dollars, the market became the epicenter of the Dark Web's illicit economy.

AlphaBay was not merely a marketplace for illegal goods but an ecosystem designed to ensure anonymity and security for buyers and sellers alike. Utilizing cryptocurrencies like Bitcoin and Monero,

the platform attracted criminals of all types, from small local gangs to major international cartels. Its user-friendly interface and advanced security measures made it accessible even to the less tech-savvy, turning it into a global phenomenon.

However, behind the apparent invincibility of the platform lay a network of human errors and vulnerabilities that ultimately led to its downfall. The collapse of AlphaBay in July 2017 marked a pivotal moment in the fight against online black markets, proving that even the most sophisticated networks are not immune to justice.

How AlphaBay Operated

A Sophisticated Ecosystem

AlphaBay stood out among other Dark Web marketplaces for its complexity and technical sophistication. The site was designed to ensure security and anonymity for both buyers and sellers, making it an

ideal hub for all kinds of illicit transactions.

Access and Registration: Accessing the platform required using the Tor browser, which ensured user anonymity. After registration, each user had to set up a PGP (Pretty Good Privacy) key to encrypt communications, adding an additional layer of security.

Use of Cryptocurrencies: AlphaBay supported Bitcoin and Monero as payment methods. While Bitcoin was widely used, Monero offered even greater anonymity due to its advanced privacy features, making transactions nearly impossible to trace.

Advanced User Interface: Unlike many other Dark Web marketplaces, AlphaBay featured a user-friendly interface with advanced search functions, seller reviews, and a dedicated FAQ section for newcomers. This approach made it accessible even to less tech-savvy users.

Feedback and Reputation: The feedback system allowed buyers to rate sellers, similar to legitimate platforms like eBay. This encouraged sellers to maintain high standards, fostering trust among users.

Support and Moderation: AlphaBay had a team of moderators who handled disputes between buyers and sellers. Additionally, customer support addressed technical questions, making the platform professional and reliable for its users.

Categories of Goods and Services

AlphaBay was renowned for the variety of goods and services available. The main categories included:

Drugs: One of the most popular sections, offering every type of narcotic, from cannabis to synthetic substances.

Weapons: Guns, rifles, and ammunition were available, although logistical challenges limited their shipping.

Stolen Data: Personal information, credit card numbers, and login credentials were among the best-selling items.

Fake Documents: Fake driver's licenses, passports, and certificates were offered with quality guarantees.

Hacking Services: From DDoS attacks to custom malware, hacking services were in high demand.

Security and Anonymity

AlphaBay implemented advanced security measures to protect its users:

Encryption: All communications and transactions were encrypted using PGP keys.

Escrow: The escrow system ensured that funds were held until the buyer confirmed receipt of the product or service.

Decentralized Servers: The platform utilized distributed servers to prevent a

single seizure from compromising the entire system.

AlphaBay represented a near-perfect model of a digital black market. However, its complexity and the sheer volume of transactions attracted the attention of law enforcement, who began monitoring its activities, ultimately leading to its downfall.

Goods for Sale: A Market Without Rules

An Unprecedented Assortment

AlphaBay was renowned for the breadth of its offerings, covering virtually every type of illegal goods and services imaginable. The platform was structured to make it easy for buyers to find what they were looking for, with clearly defined categories and an advanced search engine that simplified navigation.

Main Categories of Goods and Services

Drugs:

AlphaBay was the premier hub for drug trafficking on the Dark Web. The platform hosted a vast range of narcotics, from lighter substances like cannabis and MDMA to more dangerous drugs like heroin, cocaine, and fentanyl.

Vendors often provided detailed descriptions of their products, including origin, purity, and shipping methods. Buyer reviews and feedback helped create a trust system between parties.

Firearms and Ammunition:

Although less prominent than the drug section, AlphaBay offered a selection of guns, rifles, ammunition, and accessories. Some vendors even advertised customized or smuggled weapons.

Shipping firearms posed significant logistical challenges, but vendors used

advanced concealment techniques to avoid detection.

Stolen Data:

One of the most lucrative categories, the data market included credit card numbers, login credentials, corporate databases, and personal information.

These data were often purchased by hackers and cybercriminals to perpetrate further crimes like fraud and identity theft.

Fake Documents:

Driver's licenses, passports, visas, and other counterfeit documents were among the most sought-after items. Vendors guaranteed high-quality counterfeits that were nearly indistinguishable from genuine documents.

Some even provided tutorials on how to use the documents safely to avoid detection.

Hacking Services:

AlphaBay was a haven for those seeking customized hacking services. Users could purchase malware, ransomware, on-demand DDoS attacks, and even spyware.

Some vendors offered tutorials and consultations on using these tools, expanding the market to beginners.

A Market Without Moral Limits

AlphaBay was a place where morality was entirely absent, and money was the sole driver of transactions. Buyers could even find services and goods that defied imagination, such as human organs (though these listings were often scams), homemade explosives, and even contracts for murder-for-hire.

Impact on Global Crime

Thanks to its global reach and ease of use, AlphaBay transformed organized crime. It allowed small-time criminals to access

resources previously reserved for major cartels, increasing the accessibility of crime to anyone with an internet connection.

This "supermarket of crime" not only expanded the global black market but also changed how crimes were conceived and executed in the digital age.

The Founder: Alexandre Cazes and His Downfall

Who Was Alexandre Cazes

Alexandre Cazes, the founder of AlphaBay, was a young Canadian tech entrepreneur who presented himself as a computer genius and a successful businessman. Born in 1991, Cazes showed extraordinary talent for programming and technology from a young age. However, his passion for innovation intertwined with an insatiable ambition, leading him to create one of the largest digital black markets ever known.

Known online by aliases such as "Alpha02," Cazes managed to maintain a low profile despite his growing wealth. Living a life of luxury in Thailand, he owned luxury cars, villas, and an estimated multimillion-dollar fortune. However, all of this was built on a network of illicit transactions that quickly drew the attention of international law enforcement agencies.

Cazes' Double Life

While publicly appearing as a successful expatriate, his secret life was deeply tied to the world of online crime. Cazes ran AlphaBay with almost corporate-like professionalism, implementing policies, support systems, and security measures that made the platform one of the most reliable marketplaces on the Dark Web.

Discreet Leadership: Cazes communicated with his team members through encrypted

channels, minimizing the risk of being identified.

An Empire Built on Crime: Thanks to transaction fees and vendor commissions, AlphaBay generated enormous profits, solidifying Cazes as one of the most influential figures on the Dark Web.

Fatal Errors

Despite his intelligence and attention to detail, Cazes made several critical mistakes that led to his identification and capture.

Unencrypted Documents: During a search of his devices, authorities discovered an unprotected file containing passwords and details related to AlphaBay's management.

Personal Emails: Some ads posted on AlphaBay included a personal email address Cazes had used years earlier for legitimate purposes.

Lavish Lifestyle: His extravagant spending on luxury goods in Thailand attracted attention, making it difficult to maintain anonymity.

The Arrest and Its Aftermath

In July 2017, Cazes was arrested at his residence in Thailand during a coordinated operation involving the FBI, Europol, and Thai authorities. Within days, AlphaBay's servers were seized, marking the end of the marketplace.

Cazes was found dead in his cell shortly after his arrest, in what authorities declared a suicide. His death raised numerous questions but did not halt the investigations that led to further arrests of AlphaBay collaborators and users.

Cazes' Legacy

The story of Alexandre Cazes serves as an example of how greed and excess can lead to

ruin. Despite his extraordinary technical abilities, his criminal empire could not withstand the scrutiny of international authorities, proving that no one is truly safe in the world of digital crime.

Investigations and the Shutdown of AlphaBay

The Beginning of the Investigation

The investigation into AlphaBay began when authorities noticed a significant increase in criminal activities linked to the Dark Web. Initial suspicions arose from reports of suspicious cryptocurrency transactions and the widespread availability of illegal goods such as drugs, weapons, and stolen data. Law enforcement agencies, including the FBI, DEA, and Europol, focused their efforts on AlphaBay, identifying it as the largest digital black market of its time.

Advanced Investigative Techniques

The dismantling of AlphaBay required the use of advanced investigative techniques and close international collaboration. Law enforcement adopted several strategies to gather evidence and identify the platform's administrators and users:

Cryptocurrency Tracing: Investigators used blockchain analysis software to monitor Bitcoin and Monero transactions. Despite anonymity measures, user errors allowed authorities to link transactions to real identities.

Platform Infiltration: Undercover agents registered on AlphaBay to purchase illegal goods, gathering information on its operations and system vulnerabilities.

International Cooperation: Agencies from multiple countries collaborated to share data and coordinate actions, leveraging tools like Europol's Joint Cybercrime Action Taskforce.

Server Identification: Investigators pinpointed AlphaBay's servers through configuration errors made by the administrators. These servers contained a wealth of information, including transactions and user communications.

The Day of the Shutdown

On July 5, 2017, AlphaBay was officially shut down during a coordinated international operation. Thai authorities arrested Alexandre Cazes at his residence in Bangkok, while the FBI and other agencies seized servers located in various parts of the world.

Data Seizure: The operation recovered massive amounts of data, including user information, transactions, and vendor details.

Global Arrests: In addition to Cazes, dozens of users and collaborators of the platform were arrested in multiple countries.

Global Consequences

The shutdown of AlphaBay marked a turning point in the fight against Dark Web black markets:

Impact on Illegal Markets: The closure of AlphaBay left a significant void, temporarily reducing online illicit activities.

Adoption of Advanced Security Measures: Subsequent markets learned from AlphaBay's mistakes, adopting more sophisticated anonymity and security measures.

Strengthened International Cooperation: The case highlighted the importance of a global approach to tackling online crime, leading to new initiatives for monitoring the Dark Web.

The fall of AlphaBay was a significant victory but also a reminder of the ongoing challenges in combating digital crime in an ever-evolving world.

Legal and Social Consequences

Trials and Sentences

The shutdown of AlphaBay led to a series of trials around the world, marking a crucial moment in the fight against online crime. The defendants included not only the founder, Alexandre Cazes, but also active sellers and buyers who had used the platform for illegal purposes.

Severe Sentences: Many of those involved received exemplary penalties, with sentences ranging from 10 years to life imprisonment, depending on the severity of their crimes.

Asset Seizures: Authorities confiscated millions of dollars in cryptocurrencies and luxury goods belonging to the market's key players, significantly reducing the profits of organized crime.

Global Implications: Some of the most significant trials took place in the United States and Europe, with investigations

leading to the arrest of new suspects even years after the site's closure.

Impact on the Dark Web

The fall of AlphaBay had a significant impact on the Dark Web ecosystem, creating a temporary disruption in illicit markets and influencing how subsequent platforms were developed.

Power Vacuum: The sudden shutdown left a void in the digital black market, prompting users to migrate to alternative platforms like Dream Market and Hansa Market.

Evolution of Security Measures: Subsequent markets adopted more advanced security protocols to avoid AlphaBay's mistakes, making it harder for authorities to identify users and administrators.

Temporary Decline in Illicit Activities: In the months immediately following the shutdown, a decline in transactions on the

Dark Web was observed, demonstrating the operation's direct impact.

Social and Legal Effects

Beyond its impact on organized crime, the AlphaBay case raised public awareness of the dangers of the Dark Web and highlighted the need for new policies to combat online crimes.

New Legislation: Many countries introduced stricter regulations to monitor cryptocurrency transactions and strengthen laws against illicit digital markets.

Education and Awareness: Authorities and non-governmental organizations launched campaigns to inform the public about the risks of the Dark Web and promote greater vigilance.

Enhanced Collaboration: The success of the operation underscored the importance of international cooperation, leading to the

creation of task forces dedicated to monitoring online criminal activities.

A Warning for the Future

The story of AlphaBay serves as a warning to digital criminals, demonstrating that even the most sophisticated platforms can be dismantled through determination and collaboration among authorities. However, the case also highlights the resilient nature of organized crime, which continues to evolve to evade justice. The fight against online crime remains a complex and ever-changing challenge, requiring constant effort from governments, law enforcement, and civil society.

Conclusion: AlphaBay and the Evolution of Online Crime

The shutdown of AlphaBay stands as one of the most significant operations in the fight against digital crime, marking a

turning point in the history of illicit Dark Web markets. This case not only demonstrated the vulnerability of even the most sophisticated online platforms but also underscored the importance of international collaboration and advanced technologies in investigations.

AlphaBay was more than just a black market; it was an ecosystem reflecting the complexity and resilience of organized crime in the digital age. Its fall left a void but also triggered a process of adaptation and innovation in subsequent markets, highlighting that the battle against online crime is a constant game of evolution.

A Lesson for the Future

The story of AlphaBay offers important lessons for authorities and civil society:

The Resilience of Organized Crime: Despite successes, digital crime continues to find new ways to thrive, exploiting

technological and societal vulnerabilities.

The Need for a Global Approach: International cooperation remains essential to tackling challenges that transcend national borders.

The Importance of Education and Awareness: Only through greater knowledge of the risks associated with the Dark Web can we hope to reduce demand for such markets.

AlphaBay will remain in history as a symbol of the power and perils of technology. While its fall represents a significant victory, it also serves as a reminder of the importance of staying vigilant and adaptable in the face of digital crime challenges.

The Cannibal Cop: When Fantasy Challenges Reality

Introduction: The Beginning of a Nightmare

It was an ordinary day when the life of Gilberto Valle, a New York City police officer, took a drastic turn. Valle, a devoted husband and affectionate father, suddenly found himself under intense media scrutiny in one of the most disturbing cases of the digital age. Authorities discovered that Valle had been leading a double life online, frequenting forums on the Dark Web where he discussed abduction, torture, and cannibalism.

The revelation came to light in 2012 when Valle's wife discovered explicit chats and meticulously detailed plans on their home computer, outlining scenarios to kidnap and kill women. The content was so graphic and horrifying that she reported her husband to

the authorities. What followed was an investigation that not only led to Valle's arrest but also sparked a national debate about freedom of thought, privacy, and the fine line between fantasy and crime.

Dubbed "The Cannibal Cop" by the media, Gilberto Valle's story exposed the dark underbelly of the Dark Web, a place where anonymity provides refuge for forbidden and sometimes dangerous fantasies. But was he truly a criminal, or was he a man ensnared by the depths of his mind, unable to separate imagination from intent? This case remains an enigma, challenging justice and morality in contemporary society.

Gilberto Valle: The Public and Secret Lives

An Ordinary Man with an Extraordinarily Dark Side

Gilberto Valle, born and raised in New York, appeared to epitomize normalcy. The son of immigrants, he attended public schools in the city and earned a degree in

criminology from the University of Maryland. A career with the New York Police Department seemed like a natural choice—a path he pursued to ensure safety and stability for his family. Valle was described by colleagues as a competent officer, respectful and dedicated to his work.

Outside of work, Gilberto was a loving husband and devoted father. Married to Kathleen, he lived a seemingly peaceful life in a New York suburb, spending his free time with his wife and their infant daughter. Nothing in his public life hinted at the existence of a parallel reality so deeply disturbing.

The Double Life Online

Behind this façade of normalcy, however, Valle cultivated a secret life in the dark world of the Dark Web. Using aliases, he frequented forums where he shared graphic fantasies about kidnapping, torture, and

cannibalism. These online spaces, characterized by anonymity and a lack of regulation, provided an environment where Valle could freely explore his darkest thoughts.

Macabre Chats: The conversations found on his computer were explicit and detailed. Valle discussed elaborate plans to abduct women, some of whom were people he knew in real life. Names, photos, and addresses of potential victims were included in his notes.

Lists of Victims: Documents on his computer contained personal information about women Valle had identified as potential targets. Among them were friends of his wife and colleagues from work.

A Blurred Line Between Fantasy and Reality

The discovery of his online activities immediately raised unsettling questions. Was Valle merely exploring dark fantasies, or did he have real intentions of acting on

these plans? The boundary between thought and action became the focal point of the legal and moral debates that followed.

An Obsessive Mind: Experts called to testify during the trial described Valle as a man trapped in compulsive fantasies, unable to clearly distinguish between the imaginary and the real.

The Defense of Free Thought: Valle's attorneys argued that, however disturbing, his thoughts did not constitute a crime without concrete evidence of an attempt to act.

Gilberto Valle's public life was an unsettling paradox: a man who protected his community by day but immersed himself in a world of darkness and forbidden desires by night. This duality remains one of the most fascinating and disturbing aspects of the case.

The Discovery of Dark Fantasies

A Computer Hiding Disturbing Secrets

The turning point in the case of Gilberto Valle came in 2012 when his wife Kathleen, concerned about changes in her husband's behavior, decided to check his computer. What she discovered surpassed her worst fears: a trove of explicit chats and detailed plans to abduct, torture, and even cannibalize women. Some of the potential victims were real people, including family friends and work colleagues.

Shocking Chats: Valle's online conversations, conducted primarily on Dark Web forums, included graphic descriptions of violent acts. Using aliases, he discussed elaborate plans to kidnap women with other users.

Lists of Victims: Documents found on his computer listed names, photos, and addresses of women Valle considered potential targets. These lists suggested a level of planning that made it difficult to

categorize his activities as mere fantasies.

Online Searches: Authorities discovered that Valle had researched restraint tools, poisons, and methods to avoid detection, further fueling suspicions about his intent to act on his plans.

Kathleen Reports Her Husband

Horrified by these discoveries, Kathleen immediately contacted the FBI, handing over her husband's computer as evidence. The ensuing investigation revealed a broader network of individuals sharing similar interests on the Dark Web. However, Valle became the public face of this dark underworld, attracting media and public attention.

A Case That Raises Disturbing Questions

The discovery of Valle's activities led to several critical questions:

Fantasy or Real Intent? Defense attorneys argued that, however disturbing, the chats were mere fantasies and did not constitute a crime without concrete actions to carry them out.

Freedom of Expression: The case raised issues about the boundary between the right to free thought and the risk of planning real crimes.

The Role of the Dark Web: The case highlighted how the Dark Web can serve as a space to explore taboo thoughts, but also how it can be used to plan illegal actions.

The revelation of Gilberto Valle's dark fantasies shed light on a hidden and unsettling world where the line between imagination and crime becomes dangerously blurred. This central element of the case became the focal point of the trial and the ensuing legal debates.

The Dark Web as a Haven for Forbidden Fantasies

A Space Without Rules

The Dark Web, with its promise of anonymity and lack of regulation, has become a haven for those wishing to explore forbidden fantasies or discuss taboo topics. While it is primarily known for illegal activities like drug trafficking and the sale of stolen data, the Dark Web also serves as a space where dark thoughts and dangerous desires can find an audience willing to discuss them without judgment.

In Gilberto Valle's case, the Dark Web provided a platform where he could share his darkest fantasies with others. This environment allowed Valle and his interlocutors to create a virtual community where societal norms did not apply.

The Illusion of Anonymity: The Dark Web enables users to hide their identities using tools like Tor and encryption. This anonymity is one of the main reasons people

feel free to openly discuss even their most extreme thoughts.

Normalization of Fantasies: In these forums, desires and thoughts that would be considered aberrant in the real world are discussed as though they are normal. This process of "normalization" can amplify compulsive behaviors.

A Fine Line Between Thought and Action

Valle's case raised a critical question: how far can activities on the Dark Web be considered mere fantasies? While many might argue that discussing dark thoughts does not constitute a crime, others point out that these platforms can act as fertile ground for planning real crimes.

Mutual Influence: Online discussions can reinforce an individual's desires, turning what was initially a fantasy into a potential reality.

Lack of Moral Barriers: Without the usual social or legal consequences, users may feel emboldened to explore and plan actions they would never consider in the real world.

The Debate on Freedom of Expression

A central theme that emerged during Valle's trial was the right to freedom of thought and expression. While it is true that everyone has the right to explore their imagination, where should the line be drawn when these fantasies involve the planning of violent acts?

The Role of Authorities: Law enforcement must balance protecting individual freedoms with preventing crimes. Monitoring the Dark Web without violating fundamental rights remains a complex challenge.

Privacy Risks: Tools used to identify suspicious activities on the Dark Web can

also invade the privacy of users who have committed no crimes.

The Dark Web represents an ambiguous territory where the line between thought and action is often blurred. In Gilberto Valle's case, this virtual space amplified his fantasies, raising important questions about how society should address such phenomena.

The Investigation and Arrest

The Wife's Role and the Initial Discovery

The investigation into Gilberto Valle's case began when Kathleen, his wife, discovered disturbing material on his computer and decided to report it to the FBI. The federal agency took her complaint seriously, launching a thorough investigation that would uncover even more chilling details.

Access to the Computer: Investigators obtained a warrant to search Valle's

computer, recovering thousands of files, including explicit chats, victim lists, and online searches about abduction and torture methods.

International Collaboration: Due to the nature of the Dark Web, the FBI collaborated with cybersecurity experts and authorities from other countries to analyze communications and trace Valle's correspondents.

The Arrest

In 2012, Valle was arrested on charges of conspiracy to kidnap women and unauthorized use of police databases to obtain information on potential victims. The evidence collected from his computer was deemed sufficient to proceed with the arrest and formal charges.

Conspiracy: Investigators argued that Valle had crossed the line between fantasy and real planning, using police databases to gather information on specific targets.

Overwhelming Evidence: The lists of names, addresses, and personal details of potential victims suggested a level of premeditation that could not be ignored.

Public Reactions

News of Valle's arrest spread rapidly, capturing national and international media attention. The press dubbed him "The Cannibal Cop," creating an atmosphere of shock and disbelief within the community.

Impact on Family: Kathleen filed for divorce and took measures to protect their daughter, distancing herself completely from Valle.

Divided Public Opinion: While some condemned Valle as a danger to society, others raised questions about the nature of the charges, wondering if it was fair to criminalize thoughts and fantasies without concrete actions.

Implications of the Investigation

Gilberto Valle's case laid the groundwork for legal and moral debates on freedom of thought and preventive action by authorities. It also highlighted the potential dangers of the Dark Web as a platform for discussing and, in some cases, planning crimes.

The investigation served as a significant example of how technology and anonymity can be used dangerously, raising questions about the responsibility of law enforcement to balance privacy protection with the prevention of potential threats.

The Trial: Guilty of Thought or Crime?

The Beginning of the Trial

The trial of Gilberto Valle began in 2013 and garnered massive media attention due to the controversial nature of the case. The central debate revolved around a fundamental question: Was Valle guilty of

a real crime, or was he merely exploring disturbing fantasies?

The Prosecution's Case

The prosecution presented a strong case against Valle, arguing that his online actions went far beyond mere fantasy:

Conspiracy to Kidnap: The prosecution argued that the chats and victim lists indicated concrete planning, suggesting that Valle intended to carry out his plans.

Misuse of Police Databases: Valle was accused of breaking the law by using police resources to obtain personal information about his potential victims.

Disturbing Evidence: Chats were presented in which Valle discussed specific details about how to kidnap and kill women, supporting the idea that he was transitioning from fantasy to action.

The Defense Strategy

Valle's defense team based their arguments on the right to freedom of thought and expression, maintaining that their client had not committed any criminal acts:

No Concrete Action: The defense emphasized that Valle had never acted on any of the plans discussed in his chats, making his words insufficient to prove real criminal intent.

Disturbing but Not Illegal Fantasies: The attorneys described the chats as an exploration of dark fantasies, however unsettling, rather than evidence of conspiracy.

Distinction Between Thought and Action: The defense insisted that criminalizing thoughts without concrete actions would set a dangerous precedent.

The Jury's Decision

After weeks of intense testimony and debate, the jury delivered a guilty verdict, convicting Valle of conspiracy to kidnap. However, this verdict was later overturned by a federal judge, who ruled that the evidence was insufficient to prove that Valle genuinely intended to carry out his plans.

Recognition of Fantasies: The judge acknowledged that, while disturbing, Valle's online activities fell within the realm of fantasy and did not constitute a concrete crime.

Release: Valle was released after spending approximately 21 months in prison, but his life and reputation were irreparably damaged.

A Case That Divides Public Opinion

Gilberto Valle's trial raised a series of legal and moral questions that continue to divide public opinion:

Where to Draw the Line Between Fantasy and Crime? The case highlighted the complexity of judging a person's intentions based solely on words and thoughts.

Freedom of Thought vs. Public Safety: The debate over how far authorities should go to prevent crimes without violating fundamental rights remains unresolved.

The Role of the Dark Web: The case shed light on how these platforms can act as catalysts for dangerous fantasies, raising questions about their monitoring and control.

Gilberto Valle's trial remains one of the most controversial cases of the digital era, an emblematic example of how technology complicates the distinction between thought, intent, and action.

Legal and Moral Implications

An Unprecedented Case

The trial of Gilberto Valle highlighted unique legal and moral challenges, raising crucial questions about the fine line between thought, expression, and crime. While the law typically focuses on concrete actions, Valle's case posed a fundamental question: can a person's intentions be judged solely based on their thoughts or words?

Criminalizing Thought: Valle's initial conviction sparked heated debates about how far authorities can go to prevent potential crimes without violating freedom of thought. If dark thoughts are not translated into actions, do they still constitute a crime?

The Question of Intent: The evidence against Valle, while disturbing, lacked concrete actions that demonstrated an ongoing plan. This led many to question how

criminal intent is defined in the digital context.

The Role of the Dark Web

The Dark Web was central to Valle's case, underscoring its role as an anonymous platform where individuals with taboo thoughts and desires can connect. However, this anonymity raises significant questions:

A Catalyst for Dangerous Fantasies: Online communities can encourage compulsive behaviors, providing support for thoughts that might otherwise remain unexpressed in the real world.

The Challenge of Monitoring: Authorities face significant difficulties in monitoring suspicious activities on the Dark Web without violating user privacy.

Implications for Justice and Society

Valle's case also raised broader concerns about justice and society in the digital age:

Prevention vs. Individual Rights: How can law enforcement balance the need to prevent crimes with the protection of fundamental rights?

The Evolution of Law: The case highlighted the need to update laws to address the complexities of digital crime while ensuring that dangerous precedents are not set.

Education and Awareness: Society must confront the role of the Dark Web and work to educate people about the risks associated with these platforms.

An Open Question

The case of Gilberto Valle remains an emblematic example of how technology has complicated the dynamics between thought,

intent, and action. While representing a victory for the legal system in adapting to new challenges, the case has left fundamental questions unanswered about how to address similar phenomena in the future.

The legal and moral implications of the case continue to resonate, prompting jurists, lawmakers, and society to reflect on how to balance individual freedoms and collective security in an increasingly digital world.

Conclusion: A Fine Line Between Thought and Crime

The case of Gilberto Valle, better known as "The Cannibal Cop," has sparked an unprecedented debate about how law and society should address the complexities of thought, intent, and action in the digital age. While some viewed Valle as an imminent danger, others defended his right to freedom of thought, emphasizing the absence of concrete actions.

A Case That Defines an Era

Technology as a Challenge: Valle's story highlights how technology can blur the line between what is imagined and what is real. The Dark Web, with its promise of anonymity, has made it even harder to distinguish between what is protected by freedom of expression and what constitutes a real threat.

Enduring Implications: This case will continue to influence legal and moral discussions, forcing lawmakers to confront the need to balance public safety with individual rights.

An Open Question

Valle's case represents an enigma for contemporary justice. On one hand, it demonstrates the necessity of preventing potential threats; on the other, it highlights the danger of criminalizing

thoughts that, however disturbing, never materialized into actions. Society, law enforcement, and legislators must continue to reflect on how to handle similar situations in the future.

Ultimately, the case of Gilberto Valle stands as a cautionary tale for the digital world: a fine line separates thought from action, and finding the right balance will remain one of the greatest challenges of our time.

A Reflection on the Digital Darkness

1. Reflections on the Dark Web

The Dark Web represents a unique technological paradox: born as a tool to ensure privacy and freedom of expression, it has evolved into fertile ground for criminal activities. This shadowy digital space has become a haven for those seeking anonymity, but also a platform for organized crime, exploitation, and illicit transactions.

What makes the Dark Web both fascinating and unsettling is its dual nature. On one hand, it is a place where journalists, activists, and citizens in oppressive regimes can exercise their right to free speech and protect their identities. On the other hand, it is the stage for acts that defy every moral and legal boundary.

This contradiction is not just technological but deeply human. The Dark Web reflects the most extreme facets of our nature: the pursuit of freedom and the temptation of the illicit. Exploring it means grappling with complex questions about our relationship with technology and how it amplifies both the best and the worst of humanity.

2. The Impact on Society and Justice

The Dark Web has posed unprecedented challenges to both society and the justice system. On one hand, it represents a significant threat to global security, providing a space where organized crime and illicit activities can thrive. On the other, it raises fundamental questions about protecting individual rights and using technology to monitor these activities.

Security vs. Privacy: The Dark Web demands a delicate balance between the need for

public safety and the necessity of protecting citizens' privacy. Monitoring technologies, while powerful, must be used cautiously to prevent abuse and ensure fundamental rights are not violated.

International Collaboration: The global nature of the Dark Web makes cooperation between nations essential to combat criminal activities. However, this collaboration faces obstacles such as differing legal frameworks and conflicting political interests.

The Dark Web has underscored the urgency for institutions to adapt to a rapidly evolving technological world, where the line between security and personal freedom grows increasingly thin. Only through constructive dialogue among governments, tech companies, and citizens can these challenges be effectively addressed.

3. A Window into the Digital Darkness

The future of the Dark Web remains shrouded in mystery, but one thing is certain: it will continue to evolve, bringing new challenges and opportunities. As technologies advance, criminal activities also adapt, developing increasingly sophisticated methods to exploit security vulnerabilities.

Potential Technological Evolutions

Artificial Intelligence and Machine Learning: These technologies could be leveraged by both law enforcement and criminals. On one hand, AI might enhance the ability to track and analyze Dark Web data; on the other, criminals could use it to create more complex and automated cyberattacks.

Blockchain and Cryptocurrencies: While cryptocurrencies provide anonymity, blockchain transaction analysis has proven useful in dismantling criminal networks.

However, the emergence of new privacy-focused cryptocurrencies poses a growing challenge.

A Collaborative Approach to Combating Crime

Addressing the threats posed by the Dark Web requires a global and concerted effort. Governments, tech companies, and international organizations must work together to:

Share Knowledge: Build a collaborative network to exchange information on emerging threats.

Invest in Research and Development: Fund advanced technologies to monitor and prevent illicit activities.

Educate New Generations: Raise awareness about the risks and the importance of using technology responsibly.

The Role of Public Awareness

An essential aspect of combating Dark Web threats is increasing public awareness. Informing people about the dangers and

dynamics of this hidden world can help reduce the demand for illicit content and services, creating a positive ripple effect on society.

The Dark Web, with all its shadows and secrets, represents a window into the darkness of the digital era. However, with collective commitment and a proactive approach, we can transform this darkness into an opportunity to build a safer and more responsible digital future.

4. Call to Action

The Dark Web is a complex reality that reflects the darkest and most controversial aspects of our digital age. However, it is not an inevitable fate; with awareness and commitment, it is possible to mitigate the risks it poses and promote ethical use of technology.

What We Can Do as Individuals

Educate Ourselves: Knowledge is our most powerful weapon. Learning how the Dark Web works, understanding its dangers, and recognizing warning signs can make a significant difference.

Promote Responsible Technology Use: Every user has the power to positively influence the digital landscape by adopting ethical behaviors and encouraging others to do the same.

Report Suspicious Activities: Collaboration with authorities can help combat criminal activities. Reporting what seems out of place is an important step in protecting the community.

The Role of Institutions and Tech Companies

Invest in Security: Companies must develop advanced tools and technologies to monitor and prevent illicit activities on the Dark Web.

Collaborate Globally: Governments and organizations need to join forces to address threats that transcend national borders.

Support Ethical Regulation: Laws and policies must balance the right to privacy with the need to ensure collective security.

Looking Ahead

The Dark Web represents an ever-evolving challenge but also an opportunity to rethink how we use technology and how we can protect ourselves from its misuse. Every person has a role to play in this fight, from choosing to stay informed to taking responsibility for action.

With a globally aware and united community, we can confront the shadows of the Dark Web and transform our digital future into a safer, fairer, and more responsible space.

Sommario